FIGHT NIGHT 1939

Joe Louis and Tony Galento square off in a posed shot at their pre-fight physical.

FIGHT NIGHT 1939

The Champ, the Challenger, and a Portrait of America on the Brink

Joseph Monninger

STEERFORTH PRESS
Lebanon, New Hampshire

This book was previously published in 2006 as
Two Ton: One Fight, One Night: Tony Galento v. Joe Louis.

This edition published in 2025

For information about permission to reproduce
selections from this book, write to:
Steerforth Press
31 Hanover Street, Suite 1
Lebanon, New Hampshire 03766

ISBN (paperback): 978-1-58642-409-1

Printed in the United States of America

EU RP (for authorities only): eucomply OÜ, Pärnu mnt. 139b-14, 11317,
Tallinn, Estonia, hello@eucompliancepartner.com, +33757690241

1 3 5 7 9 10 8 6 4 2

For Peter Johnson

"One plays football, one doesn't play boxing."

—JOYCE CAROL OATES, *On Boxing*

"Oh, I knew that if I kept on fighting, some guy would come along and take the title away from me, but not this guy, never tonight."

—JOE LOUIS

Preface

IN THE END, he lost his foot to diabetes, then his legs, and finally his life. "Two Ton" Tony Dominick Galento died on July 22, 1979, a ghost hero to the kids of Orange, New Jersey. Before the end, he wrestled octopuses for promotions, appeared as a tough in the Brando classic *On the Waterfront*, and wagered ten dollars he could eat fifty hot dogs before fighting a heavyweight match. He won the bout in four rounds, pulverizing a hapless Arthur DeKuh. He went out to dinner afterward on the ten bucks he won, the food washing down his sizable gullet on a tide of beer. He fought the dirtiest fight in the history of modern boxing against Lou Nova in Philadelphia, September 1939, and maintained such a reputation that other boxers sometimes fouled him in their rush to prove themselves equal to the street fight they had entered. In 1931 he knocked out three opponents in a single night, stopping Frankie Kits and Joe

Brian in one round each, and tossing away Paul Thierman in three. Between rounds, he drank beer.

Out of the ring he went through managers like hand towels, finishing with at least nine men who tried to arrange his business for him. Even the great Jack Dempsey, boxing immortal and Galento's manager from 1933 to 1934, could not calm him. Galento lived as he fought, a bus wreck, a cracked window. Days before his final major fight, a scheduled ten-rounder with Max Baer, Tony's brother, Russell, asked him for a free ticket. When Tony told him to stand in line with the others, his brother threw a beer bottle at Tony's head. Bleeding from a three-inch gash on his chin, Tony had it stitched up by Doc Stern, a physician often called on to remedy Two Ton's wounds. Tony fought a few days later, the stitches removed directly before the opening bell, waddling in against Max Baer in Washington, DC. A broken knuckle stopped him that night, but the bottle wound opened too, bleeding thirty seconds into the fight.

Like Jake LaMotta, a contemporary, he tried his hand at standup comedy, played bit parts in the movies, trained on spaghetti and meatballs. He did his road work at night, saying, "I fight at night, don't I?" He made one successful comeback, knocking out Herbie Katz in the first round in 1943 and Jack Suzek in Wichita the next autumn. After fifteen years, and a 79-26-5 record, he hung up the gloves and spent the remainder of his life behind the bar of his tavern in Orange.

He is quoted in Bartlett's: "I'll moida da bum," he said. He said it often, and often of his betters.

But in the summer of 1939, on a Wednesday in June at Yankee Stadium, Two Ton Tony Galento fought Joe Louis, the finest heavyweight of his generation. The weather, cloudy, with a moderate southerly wind, proved no factor for Louis. The champ, a trim six-footer at 200 pounds, had the ideal body type for a heavyweight of that era. Called the Brown Bomber, or the Dark Destroyer, Louis came to the fight in magnificent shape. Galento, on the other hand, stood a mere 5'8" and weighed a flabby 240 pounds. The heat of a New York summer did not favor him. The odds against Galento ran 6 to 1, though a Gallup poll published by the *New York Times* reported that 47 percent of the crowd pulled for Galento. Boxing fans love an underdog, and Galento, put forward as "the bum of the month" for Joe Louis to consume, fit the bill.

They fought for a $400,000 purse, a remarkable sum in 1939. Louis was promised 40 percent to Galento's 17½ percent. The gates opened at 6 PM. NBC broadcast seven preliminary four-round bouts, not one ending in a knockout. By nine o'clock J. Edgar Hoover had found his seat at ringside, as had Supreme Court Justice John McGeehan. Heavyweight Gene Tunney, John Hamilton, chairman of the Republican National Committee, Governor Bricker of Ohio, Governor Baldwin of Connecticut, Mayor LaGuardia, Governor A. Harry Moore of New Jersey, Mayor Frank Hague of Jersey City, Postmaster General James A. Farley, Governor Herbert Lehman of New York, Bill Terry, manager of the Giants, and Jack Benny were spectators. Mrs. Lillian Brooks, Joe Louis's mother, attended, as did Mary Galento, Tony's wife. New York Police Commissioner Valentine assigned six hundred patrolmen to control the crowd inside the stadium.

Across the nation, forty million people tuned in to NBC to hear a title bout, arguably a greater sporting event in the 1930s than the World Series. An estimated 24.5 million families owned a radio, adding up to eighty million potential listeners. In the summer of 1939, the thirty-three million radios in operation equaled the total number of automobiles and telephones combined. At that time, radio provided the largest audience in history to advertisers. Appearing on radio turned a man into a household name.

A contender, a man shaped like a beer barrel, a crude, raw Italian American from Orange, New Jersey, Galento contained in his left hook the elements of the American dream. Any man could be champ. His charisma stemmed from his role as representative of the underbelly of American society, and from his humor. Years later, watching Muhammad Ali talk the world into giving him a shot at the title, Galento claimed to be the original master of ballyhoo, the first boxer to understand fully the usefulness of humor and braggadocio. The fraud, of course, is seldom a fraud to himself, and deep in his heart Galento believed he could defeat the Brown Bomber.

A palooka, a thug, a vibrant appetite of a man, he scrapped his way out of the streets and into the brightest light in American life. For two splendid seconds he stood on the canvas at Yankee Stadium, the great Joe Louis stretched out beneath him, champ of the world, the toughest man alive, the mythical hero of the waterfront, of New Jersey, of an American nation little more than a year away from war. "I'll moida da bum," he'd predicted. And though Joe Louis was no bum, Two Ton Tony had been as good as his word.

1

"FETCH" IS THE DISTANCE over which wind works on water: the longer the fetch, the greater the wave-building action. On a typical New Jersey summer day, the fetch stirs from the Carolinas, blowing northward along the coast, bringing humidity and coolness off the ocean for a mile or two inland. On certain days in June, a marine layer, extending halfway across the state, keeps the ocean counties of New Jersey cool while the inland cities and boroughs swelter. By eleven o'clock most mornings a sea breeze begins, fueled by the cooler ocean air streaming inland to replace the rapidly rising heated air over the land. When the two small fronts meet and neutralize one another, the day can become unbearably cloying, a glued heat touching everything, the air trapped in the small leaves of garden hosta and Japanese maples, the roadways turning to tar and shimmering waves of lilac gasoline spills.

* * *

ON WEDNESDAY, June 28, 1939, the weather hung close to the ground. Clouds stalled and turned the sun soft. With little wind, the sound of bees and blue jays seemed louder than usual. Later in the day, when the heat began to lift, forty million people around the United States tuned in to listen as Joe Louis, the Brown Bomber, defended his title against Tony Galento, tavernkeeper from Orange, New Jersey. Most of the nation, and a good portion of the world, halted for eleven minutes. The sound of the fight would play in sausage palaces in Orange and Asbury Park, in groceries throughout Harlem and along Lennox Street. It would play beside the 1,216-acre ash pile in Flushing Meadows that was reclaimed for the 1939 World's Fair, and it would play beside the slender, 610-foot Trylon, a triangular male phallus, and its companion, the 200-foot-wide Perisphere, global and ripe, as they declared the fair open to technology, to hope, to the future. Without intended irony, Henry Dreyfuss, a visionary architect, exhibited in Perisphere a municipal plan labeled "Democracity," a business and cultural hub called "Centertron," both entities surrounded by bedroom communities of ten thousand called "Pleasantvilles" — and the fight found people there. Exhibits of RCA's first commercial television, and the 1940 Crosley, a small, sixty-miles-to-the-gallon automobile, underlined the fair's Dawn of a New Day theme. To demonstrate the materials that would go into the "house of tomorrow," a building crew constructed a residence each day and tore it down at night, the better to reveal the modern materials used to create a new building scheme. The foreman, reporters joked, faced firing if he ever completed the job. As he worked with the night crew, he listened to the fight.

Girls carrying cotton candy along the Jersey shore would pull their boyfriend's hands to keep going, to get away from the radio, to stop listening and pay attention. It was just a fight, the girls said. But the sound of the fight proved inescapable; it stretched from one block to the next, from one grab to the next, spreading the fight from ear to ear with painful intermissions as one released one broadcast to catch the next.

Black men arranged on front stoops listened to the announcer's description pushing through into the open street, into the night, and into their memories. Joe Louis fought for them, they understood, and for every damn sharecropping nigger in the country. King Joe had already defeated Max Schmeling, his sorest test. They sometimes raised their fists as they listened and fought beside Joe Louis, their shoulders dipping and rising for leverage like teeter-totters.

IN THE *New York Times* on the morning of the fight, Eleanor Roosevelt answered Miss Florence Birmingham, "a slender, somber-dressed president of the Massachusetts Women's Political Club," who had sponsored legislation aimed at keeping women out of Massachusetts public posts. Miss Birmingham felt women should not hold jobs outside the home, but Mrs. Roosevelt asked, "Do you want us to become a fascist nation which tells one when to work and how? As soon as you discriminate against one group that discrimination very often cannot be controlled and spreads to others." Miss Birmingham had charged that childless working wives formed a new plutocracy and posed a grave threat to the American system of government.

In the same edition, the real estate listings carried an ad for seasonal rentals on Lake Waramug, Connecticut, consisting of a five-room lodge with fieldstone fireplaces, two hours from Manhattan for $400. A summer cabin rental on Ossippee Lake, Maine, went for $20 a week. For $18,000 one could purchase in the heart of a lovely New England village a "genuine Colonial, 9 rooms, 3 baths, open fireplaces, oil burner, electric refrigerator, barn, garage, nearly four acres, fruit trees, and a brook."

A REPORTER for the *Times* wrote on the day of the fight that the massive crowds visiting the fair each day naturally moved to the right after passing through the turnstiles. The reporter had responded to claims by vendors who set up on the left of the turnstiles that their business receipts totaled half of what their neighbors on the opposite side of the turnstiles tallied. One concessionaire sought to prove his point by checking the totals on a right and left turnstile. Right: 146,688. Left: 101,696. While fair psychologists had difficulty explaining the phenomena, an old time showman saw nothing remarkable in the discrepancy. "No reason," the old showman said, "why they shouldn't use both sides, but they just won't." He labeled it human instinct, one that any good showman uses to his advantage. The reporter watched the turnstiles for an hour and asserted the fair worker had known his business.

Foot traffic at the World's Fair remained a concern, especially given that Fair Corporation president, Grover Whalen, warned that sixty thousand children under the age of twelve would get lost while visiting. He based his estimate on fifty million tourists attending the fair, and extrapolated from past statistics on fair-going. The same fifty million, translated to dollars, represented the value of the concessions program, a deal cornered by Coca-Cola. The soft drink company planned to sell its drinks for five cents a bottle.

LOUIS ARMSTRONG'S "Jeepers Creepers" played on the radio, brought into people's homes on the new FM airwaves, a development put into place a few months earlier. Radios played "South of the Border, Down Mexico Way," by Jimmy Kennedy, and "Three Little Fishies (Itty Bitty Poo)" by Saxie Dowell, and "I Get Along Without You Very Well (Except Sometimes)" by Hoagie Carmichael, lyrics by Jane Brown Thompson. The music played around the soft spill of sprinklers coming on and around the hiss of hoses spraying asphalt and white walls. Kids played buck-buck, and stoopball, and cops and robbers. After dinner people sat on screen porches and watched the fireflies, or turned on a light and read Raymond Chandler's *The Big Sleep*, or John P. Marquand's *Wickford Point*, or Henry Miller's *Tropic of Capricorn*, or Katherine Porter's *Pale Horse, Pale Rider*, or Dalton Trumbo's *Johnny Got His Gun*, or Nathaniel West's *Day of the Locust*, or

Thomas Wolfe's *The Web and the Rock,* or John Steinbeck's *The Grapes of Wrath.* The kids scanned the new comic strip *Superman,* which had debuted in January.

If they decided to take in a movie, as ninety million citizens did each week, they could travel to the local Rialto to see Edmund Goulding direct Bette Davis in *Dark Victory;* James Stewart and Marlene Dietrich in *Destry Rides Again;* Henry Fonda and Claudette Colbert in John Ford's *Drums along the Mohawk;* Robert Donat and Greer Garson in *Goodbye, Mr. Chips;* Vivien Leigh, Clark Gable, Leslie Howard and Olivia de Havilland in *Gone With the Wind;* Cary Grant, Victor McLaglen, Douglas Fairbanks Jr., Joan Fontaine, and Sam Jaffe in *Gunga Din;* Basil Rathbone and Nigel Bruce in *The Hound of the Baskervilles;* Charles Laughton in *The Hunchback of Notre Dame;* Irene Dunne and Charles Boyer in *Love Affair;* James Stewart and Jean Arthur in *Mr. Smith Goes to Washington;* Cary Grant and Jean Arthur in *Only Angels Have Wings;* John Wayne and Claire Trevor in *Stagecoach;* and Judy Garland, Ray Bolger, Bert Lahr, Jack Haley, and Frank Morgan in *The Wizard of Oz.*

IN THE 1938 January edition of *Women's Home Companion,* the following brands placed ads: Swift's Premium ham and bacon, Campbell's soups, Del Monte vegetables. Del Monte dried fruits, Franco-American spaghetti, Sunkist lemons, Heinz vinegar, Wheatena, Wesson Oil, Royal Baking Powder, Jelke's Good Luck Vegetable Oleomargarine, Junket Rennet Powder, Crisco.

* * *

SOMEWHERE NEAR seven o'clock Tony Galento left Orange, New Jersey, and drove two dozen or so miles to Yankee Stadium. The main event had a ten o'clock start time. He wore a beige sports shirt, open at the collar, beneath a dove sports jacket. He resembled a dad on an evening trip to the ballyard, or a fellow stopping at the neighborhood tavern before dropping his coat and playing a game of nine ball. Cameras clicked and popped as he climbed the few steps to the stadium entrance, his tread not a fat man's though he was fleshy at 240 pounds and only five-foot-eight, his mouth working a piece of chewing gum. Muscles in his forehead flexed to the movement of his jaw. He wore no hat.

OF THE TWO fighters, Galento appeared rooted and dense, while the lighter Louis skimmed into the ballpark surrounded by his usual entourage: Chappie Blackburn, Julian Black, and John Roxborough. They comprised an all-black management team that was, perhaps, an even greater marvel than the fighter himself. They had successfully guided Louis to a championship, had brought him where only one other black man, Jack Johnson, had ever gone, and they had massaged his reputation in America with infinite care.

One of the seven rules established by Julian Black and John Roxborough when they took over Louis's contract was never to be seen gloating over the sunken body of a white man. Jack Johnson had ignored such social injunctions and had paid a heavy price as a result. After winning the crown from James Braddock in 1937, black people called to Louis, "We're depending on you," "We got another chance," and "Don't be another Jack Johnson." By referring to Jack Johnson, known to the black community as L'il Artha, they warned him not to be uppity, not to be arrogant, not to be prideful like the former heavyweight champion.

Implicit in the shouts was a warning to stay away from white women. That had been part of Jack Johnson's downfall. Though the crowd didn't know it, the warning came too late for Joe Louis, who had already been entangled with several white women, even accepting an automobile — a black Buick with a mahogany bar in the back seat and whitewall tires — from one in exchange for two ringside seats, and whatever else they settled on, for the Max Baer fight a few years earlier. The public didn't know about the liaisons, not even about the one with Olympic gold medal skater Sonja Henie, or, by some rumors, with Mae West. Louis stood before the crowd without moral stain, representing, as one pastor from a small southern church wrote in a letter to him, the ideal of complete assimilation: "Some day I feel you will be the champion, and should this come to pass, try always to be the champion of your people, so that when you are no longer champion, the world will say of you — he was a black man outside, but a white man inside, most of all in his heart."

Blacks remained careful not to "jump at the sun," a common admonition against taking too much pleasure in accomplishments, and Louis, who had accomplished more than most, proved a devoted student.

In newsreels the day after the Galento fight, Joe Louis's entrance to Yankee Stadium revealed nothing more than a snap brim hat, elegant straw, disappearing down a long funnel of men lining the way for him to the locker room. One could hardly discern a man beneath the hat; it could have been carried by a breeze. In the foreground, in the streets and in the glow of car headlights pressing around the steel edifice, countless men strained to see him, all of them in hats, all of them in suit coats and hard-soled shoes.

YANKEE STADIUM was the first ballyard to be called a "stadium" — an acknowledgment of baseball's new urban identity. Built on the model of the Yale Bowl in New Haven, it it took less than an hour to get there by subway from Times Square, just across from the old Polo Grounds. It opened in the spring of 1923, but by the mid 1930s, the time of the major Louis bouts, the bleachers had been extended. The first fight held in Yankee Stadium, Leonard v. Tendler, brought in receipts of $452,648. The fight took place on a ring erected over second base.

The construction of the stadium had been a marvel. Built on farmland granted by the British to John Lion Gardiner prior to the Revolutionary War, the stadium held sixty thousand patrons, approximately the same number as the Roman Colosseum. Yankee owner Colonel Ruppert paid $600,000 to the William Waldorf Astor estate for what had been a rough lumberyard, and the final price tag ran to $2.5 million. The stadium consumed 45,000 cubic yards of earth, one million feet of Pacific Coast fir, 20,000 cubic yards of concrete, 800 tons of reinforcing steel, 2,200 tons of structural steel, 135,000 steel casings, 400,000 pieces of maple lumber, and one million brass screws. The White Construction Company commenced work in May 1922 and finished two hundred and eighty-four workdays later. The country's first electric scoreboard kept track of the lineups and out-of-town scores. The opening day program, Yankees v. Red Sox, cost fifteen cents.

The Yankee teams of that period are legendary. Ruth, Gehrig, and later DiMaggio played all summer long. Ballgame seats in the balcony sold for $2.50. As a boxing venue, Yankee Stadium proved difficult. Not only were fights subject to weather cancellation, but they could also be difficult to see.

As Galento and Louis made their way to the stadium, scalpers worked the crowd. Face value for a prime ringside ticket stood at $27.50. The cheapest bleacher seats, unreserved, went for $5.75. A smart ticket speculator could easily double his investment. Fifteen hundred foot patrolman, seven mounted sergeants in charge of seventy mounted men, and three motorcycle sergeants with thirty-nine motorcycle patrolmen and between one hundred and two hundred plainclothesmen, a public address truck, four patrol wagons, two emergency trucks, two ambulances, and two two-way radio cars surged around Yankee Stadium. Nine captains, seven lieutenants, and 128 sergeants signed on to direct the staff, all of them working under the command of Chief Inspector Louis F. Costuma and Deputy Chief Inspector James McGoey of the Bronx. Local authorities confirmed it as the most comprehensive police precaution ever taken in connection with a local fight. For the Primo Carnera–Joe Louis fight several years before, fifteen hundred patrolmen had remained on duty throughout the night, but the Galento bout promised to be bigger.

THE CONTESTANTS entered the stadium at about the same time, their schedule prescribed by a photo shoot arranged for the fifteen hundred members of the press in attendance. Stripped to shorts — Louis in dark trunks with a gold line down his hip, and Galento in a black pair, wide and cinched up his commodious gut like a paper sack around a loaf of bread — they posed for photos in mock combat, their fists inches away from one another's chin. The difference between the men was stark: Galento, still working his gum, held his arms cocked, his right coming up in a can opener, Louis fending him away with his greater reach. Tony's belly looked, according to one reporter, "like a tidal wave of mud." His hairy chest, another said, merely needed the word WELCOME shaved in it to make a perfect doormat.

These men, who are perhaps an hour away from releasing these punches, hold still so as not to blur the photos being snapped all around them. They don't smile. Men crowd around them, circle them, frame them. The still photos misrepresent the event. Only the newsreel, with its rolling celluloid, captures the tension in the positioning of their arms, the steady beat of Galento's forehead muscles as he gnashes nervously on his gum. Like watching two fighting cocks being dangled upside down and swung together in forced intimacy, you can feel their blood rise.

* * *

AFTER THE PHOTOS, Dr. William Walker of the New York Athletic Commission administered a cursory examination, checking each fighter's heart with a stethoscope. Like many of the faces in the crowd, Dr. Walker's visage appeared ancient by today's standard, a white haze of hair and a round body propped in a waistcoat in front of the two combatants. In their posture on the locker-room bench the fighters showed no sign of discomfort at such forced proximity. Both appeared oddly open to fate, like two men who had boarded a plane with the idea of taking a parachute jump, and now, an hour later, watched the flight instructor pulling open the hatch. Both understood they had to jump, but neither one wanted to examine too closely the step beyond the door.

Although a brief physical was customary before boxing matches, the checkup had greater significance for Galento. To cover themselves and the New York State Boxing Commission against liability, Commissioners Brown and Phelan insisted Tony undergo a thorough physical to determine his fitness for the Louis contest. The previous March five physicians — William Walker, Charles D. Bles, Morris Beyer, Robert Hechler, and Jules Posner — fluttered around Tony for forty-five minutes while photographers snapped photos and reporters shouted out questions. When one photographer climbed on the divan to snap a picture, General Phelan yelled, "Don't stand on the sofa! You broke it down last time." Along with his usual prattle about knocking out the champ, Galento managed to turn the physical into comedy. When he returned to the waiting room after having a private consultation with the doctors, he announced, "It's a boy!" Then, for public consumption, the doctors hooked him to a sphygmomanometer to check his blood pressure. Afterward they attached plates to both biceps and one thigh. Tony balked.

"What's this?" he asked. "First you put me in the electric chair, then you tune the radio in on station WEAF."

When a doctor looked into Two Ton's ears with an ophthalmoscope, Joe Jacobs, Galento's bombastic manager, a short, waist-coated huckster who lived inside a jungle of his own words, and who stopped speaking only to draw smoke from his great cattail cigars, conceded they observed a brain, albeit a dusty one. As soon as the doctors concluded their examination, Tony told the press he passed the test with flying colors. Commissioner Phelan refused to comment until the results of all the tests had been verified in a week's time.

Now, of course, Dr. Walker checked Galento's heart one last time before nodding his assent. The men could fight. When the cameras lowered, Galento and Louis moved apart, not rapidly, but with courtesy and averted eyes, as if each acknowledged the violence they hoped to do.

IN ORANGE, New Jersey, Frank Galento, Tony's father, sprinkled water into the quiet evening air. Years before, when Tony had started fighting, Frank had counseled against it, promising if Tony became a prizefighter it would lead inevitably to heartache. He also vowed, if Tony persisted, to boycott Tony's bouts from that point forward. He kept his promise, even on this day, and now spent the early evening with his garden, ignoring the pre-fight clamor. He did not travel to Yankee Stadium. Instead he sprayed water against the broad leaves of summer squash and into the tasseled hair of carrot tops. He sprayed the tomatoes and climbing beans and once or twice roped the water to knock a lightning bug, dragging its yellow flash toward the earth and damp soil with the heaviness of water.

NEAR FIGHT TIME the *Namphac*, a charter boat out of Brielle, New Jersey, returned to shore with a belly full of whiting, ling, and sea bass. It pulled its starboard side tight against a gray pier, backing the engines and churning the water as it halted. The fishing had been good. Two weeks before, Two Ton had chartered the boat, wagering he could catch the biggest fish out of any of the anglers on board. With the possibility of earning a mint if he beat Joe Louis, he preferred to go fishing than to train, and he had brought his entire entourage out for the day, the boat loaded with silver tubs of ice and Pabst Blue Ribbon.

Now, shortly before the fight began, the catch lay bright and surprised on the stern, a few splotches of intestines or blood staining the gunwale. Gulls banked and swarmed over the entrails the first mate flipped into the water. The birds pecked and came up with guts, their eyes sideways and suspicious.

* * *

THE PRELIMINARIES started: seven four-round bouts, none ending in a knockout. Abe Feldman drew with George Nicholson of Yonkers. A few months before fighting Louis, Galento fought this same Abe Feldman on Washington's Birthday in the Orange Bowl in Miami. Feldman repeatedly posed wearing a bathing suit in pre-fight photographs, the better, according to the sporting wags, to jump in the tank at fight time. In truth, Feldman trained in the surf, swimming and running, but he was nevertheless substandard fare for Galento, and John Lardner of the *New York Times* wrote that he had been "dug up from the grave."

"That smells to me like the breath of slander," "Yussel" Joe Jacobs said when told reporters speculated that Feldman had been exhumed to fight Two Ton. "Feldman was not even dead when we made the match, let alone buried. If rigor mortis had set in, Feldman's manager would have let me know, wouldn't he?"

In answer to why he picked Washington's Birthday for the contest, Jacobs said, "I figure that is the least we can do for Washington's memory. It will be a purely nonsectarian tribute regardless of race, creed, or color. The proceeds will go to a worthy private charity composed of Mr. Galento, Mrs. Galento, the infant Galento, and myself, though not in the order named."

Galento, asked about Washington's significance in his life, answered at length. "It is high time the South came to know and love Washington as we know and love him north of the Equator. Why can't we forget the Civil War and its petty grudges? Washington may have freed the slaves, but remember, he also invented the lightning rod. Let the North and South clasp the hand of friendship on Old Hickory's birthday and try to get there early."

No one could tell if he was joking, but the story ran regardless. Joe Jacobs and Tony Galento delighted in manufacturing news. In perhaps the most widely publicized photograph from the training camp before the Louis bout, Tony is pictured reclining on a rubdown table, hands behind his head, while Jacobs, cigar jauntily prying at his mouth, pretends to iron out his fighter's soft belly. It is a strangely intimate photograph despite its obvious absurdity, displaying the two men's comfort together. In another photograph, Tony gazes into a crystal ball, the future shining into his face. A stock photo of the time posed "One-Ton," Tony and Mary's son, drinking a beer while his dad chastely sipped a glass of milk. The milk, Tony said in a malapropism, "had to be patronized."

During sparring sessions Tony gave a running commentary describing his punches, promising to give Louis *this*, left hook, then *that*, right cross, and concluding with a karate kick in the air. A rumor circulated that he had developed a secret punch called a "triple hipper dipper" — a blow delivered with head, knee, and elbow simultaneously. It could paralyze a man, the camp declared. Crowds found him irresistible and visited his training camp in record numbers, often more than two thousand spectators crowding the lawns at Madame Bey's in Summit, New Jersey. Bey's, a quiet retreat in the Watchung Mountains, could barely contain Galento's energy. Nightly he snuck away from the camp to raid his bar in Orange, where he counted the till and engaged in nothing resembling training. Reporters followed him everywhere.

Declaring Tony unfazed by Louis's reputation for deadly punching accuracy, Yussel Jacobs released a story that Galento had once bested five thugs who tried to rob him. As if to persuade himself of his fighter's heart, Jacobs contacted Dr. William Moulton Marston, inventor of the lie detector, and asked him to administer a test to Galento to determine if the New Jersey Night Stick — as the papers sometimes called Tony — felt fear about facing Louis. Dr. Marston, incapable of distinguishing broad ballyhoo from sincere requests, was quoted at length in the papers describing the psychological examination he would perform on Tony, and detailing the vagaries of systolic blood-pressure testing. The camp greeted his scientific approach with a donkey bray.

Advance sales, stirred by so much bombast, began to climb. Mike Jacobs, the most powerful promoter of his day, a man who started out as a ticket speculator and became, by virtue of his contract with Joe Louis, the dominant behind-the-scenes figure in boxing through the 1930s, announced to the press that he had sold $150,000 worth of Annie Oakleys — tickets — and expected the final gate to rise to $400,000.

Several prominent fighters increased public interest in the fight by declaring that Tony had a genuine chance against the Brown Bomber. James Braddock, former champ and one of a select few who had put Joe Louis on the floor, gave Tony fair odds. "I haven't seen Tony in training and I am not picking him to win," Braddock said. "I do say

Galento has a chance to win, for he can punch and nobody, including Tony, knows what he is going to do next. He often leads with his right and then hits with his left and he's also rough and experienced." Braddock reminded fight prognosticators that he had been a 15 to 1 underdog when he lifted the crown from Max Baer. With a puncher of Galento's power in the ring, anything could happen.

THE ABSENCE of any knockout made the preliminaries stretch out longer than usual. Galento spent the time wrapping his own hands, an unusual custom he had adopted years before. Louis sat quietly, waiting. Now and then they heard crowd noises, or heard a boxer returning to the locker rooms. It was not the only time Galento had endured a protracted wait in Yankee Stadium. Fighting on the undercard for the first Louis–Schmeling bout, he had been sitting with the German boxer when Tom O'Rourke, an eighty-three-year-old fight promoter, dropped by to wish them luck. Others had dropped by too, including Jess Willard, whose chest hair, one reporter remarked, resembled a split sofa with the horsehair spilling out. After Willard departed, O'Rourke stayed for an hour chatting, then stopped to complain he didn't feel well.

"I know you can win, Max. You've got to be careful and use your head," O'Rourke counseled.

Moments later O'Rourke slipped off his chair and died. Initially, Schmeling's and Galento's trainers tried to persuade the boxers that the old man had merely fainted. When it became clear O'Rourke had died and that the body could not be removed until a coroner pronounced the official time and cause of death, the Schmeling team asked for a new room. None was available. The boxers remained in the room with the dead man until called to the ring to fight. Schmeling went on to defeat Louis in a remarkable demonstration of resiliency. He was still the only man to defeat Louis as a professional. Galento had been too shocked by the death of O'Rourke to handle Al Gainer, a stylish black heavyweight.

THE CROWD continued to arrive through the preliminaries. An earlier report in the *Newark Star-Eagle* had circulated that Galento had crashed into a heavy touring car two blocks from the weigh-in site. Along with his trainer and two state troopers, who were also in the automobile, Galento escaped serious injury, the report concluded. Despite attempts by both camps to correct the false report, some fans wondered if Tony would appear. No one could say for sure if the report had harmed the box office.

The afternoon papers also demonstrated worries about Galento's safety. Joe Kieran, writing in the *New York Times*, hoped for a "tender-hearted referee in the ring tonight when Two Ton Tony and Shufflin' Joe square off. If the Falstaff of Pugilism doesn't happen to hit Louis very early in the evening with a stunning blow, what the lithe Louis will do to the lumbering Galento will be just too ghastly." On a more pragmatic note, he continued,

> One argument is that Galento is about as good as any other heavyweight who could be tossed in with the

> Dark Destroyer and if Two Ton Tony wants to take a chance, that's his privilege and the United States Supreme Count will uphold him in case the military gents of the boxing commission get in the way. Another argument is that nobody can know ahead of time what will occur in a boxing bout and many a despised "outsider" has knocked a heavy favorite for a double loop. A third argument is that Galento is a big beefy fellow, prizefighting is no parlor game, he will get a chunk of money for the fight and what happens to him in the pursuit of his legitimate vocation is nobody's business or worry except his own.

Other writers, especially ones who had seen Galento fight over the years and had become fond of him, worried his heart would carry him too far. His extraordinary ability to take a pounding without going down, his "hippo waist, but lion heart" as one columnist put it, would remain in the swirl of Joe Louis's gloves too long. Quentin Reynolds, a well-known columnist and broadcaster of the time, offered 100 to 1 odds that Tony would die from the beating Joe Louis gave him.

Promoter Herman Muggsy Taylor, however, in a late interview with the *Washington Post*'s Bob Considine, had a different take. Taylor spoke quietly, according to Considine, and put it this way:

> The fellow honestly thinks he's going to win. Hell, he knows he can't hit Louis, or move around with him or box with him. He's told me more than once that mechanically Louis is the greatest thing he ever saw.

> But he'll admit all that, and still look me in the eye and say he's going to beat him. And the reason he says that is because he's absolutely convinced that Louis has a little kyoodle in him. Tony means Louis'll quit if he's hit. Tony's studied those films of the first Louis–Schmeling fight a hundred times. We were talking about it only yesterday and he said, "Listen, Herman, I know a quitting guy when I see one. Schmeling didn't knock him out. Louis just quit. He quit as much as Max Baer did. You watch. Let me land one left hook on his face or in his stomach, and he'll curl up. Maybe he won't go down just then, but you won't see much more fighting from him. He didn't fight back against Schmeling when he was nailed, did he?"

The fans churned into the stadium, the stories and articles clogging together into a useless lump. They read their ticket stubs and looked up at the seats, relieved to be free from work, from home responsibilities, from anything except the sight of two men squaring off in the ring.

IN THE STADIUM Joe Louis's mother, Lillian Brooks, took her seat. She had stated publicly that she wanted Joe to retire. She could not stand to watch him get hit. She also hated to see Joe's adversaries crushed, and often quizzed her son on the men's conditions after the fight. Not far from her, Mrs. Tony Galento, née Mary Grasso, and a band of Orange citizens poured into their spots. Many had traveled directly from Tony's tavern, where an enormous crowd of Galento supporters waited near the radio. In Orange and Newark, cars honked as they passed on the street. Little serious work had been done in days. The fight had consumed everyone. A lifelong friend of Two Ton's had developed a hair tonic that he promised to administer to Tony on fight day after the weigh-in. The tonic, a guarded secret, would harden into cement, making Galento's skull a torpedo, a battering ram impervious to Louis's blows. If Louis hit Tony on the top of the head, it would have the same effect as punching a jetty pier. Not to be outdone, another group of Orange barbers banded together and wagered $3,000 on Galento. In white barbers' jackets, Pat Corvino and Anthony Saporito appeared in the newspapers displaying the wad of money, a chunky bundle they called, oddly enough, The Spirit of the Oranges. Even Blackie, Tony's dog, grew so excited with all the commotion that he bit the leg of a bootblack. The following day the Orange Board of Health ordered the dog tied up pending further examination of the facts.

LOUIS ENTERED the ring first. Lithe and beautiful, a white terry robe — hood up — covering his body, he danced one or two steps to acknowledge the crowd. He rose up on his toes, not quite a jump, to test the spring of the ring boards beneath him. Then, like a man sitting down to work, he propped his backside on his corner stool and allowed his seconds to minister to him.

He did not look up when Galento made his entrance. Likely Louis could not see past his trainers and managers, but he doubtless heard the crowd. A Gallup poll had established that 47 percent of the nation pulled for a Galento win, and with the perversity of a fight crowd on holiday, the hoots and hollers rushed him to the ring. Galento resembled nothing so much as a headwaiter late out of the shower and not quite dressed for dinner. While Louis glided, Galento bustled. As soon as he climbed through the ropes, he crossed the ring and showed Louis his bandaged hands. Louis paid no attention, but the crowd laughed in appreciation, because Tony and his team had insinuated that Louis had used a metal bar tucked in his glove to knock out Max Schmeling. Joe Jacobs also claimed he had it on good authority that a doctor in the Polyclinic Hospital, where Schmeling received treatment after the bout, stated categorically that a human hand alone could not have caused the destruction to Schmeling's vertebrae that the medical team witnessed in the post-fight x-rays.

"I'm going to ask General Phelan to allow me to have a man in Louis's corner to examine his hands between rounds," Jacobs said days before the fight. "The movies [of the Schmeling fight] will show that Louis had something clutched in his glove. After the fight, Julian Black, Louis's manager, ran up to congratulate him and while they were shaking hands Black took the gimmick from Joe."

Jacobs declared, furthermore, that he had stipulated to General Phelan that the taped bandages on Louis's hands should be marked on top and bottom to ensure no one tampered with them after they were secured. Jacobs also requisitioned from the City Sealer of Weights and Measures a particularly sensitive scale for ringside so that the gloves could be weighed before and after the bout.

Having reminded everyone of those absurd accusations by showing Louis his hands, Tony scrambled back to his corner, his body busy, his nervousness apparent. Members of the crowd laughed again and nudged their neighbors, seeing Tony for the first time. To think that this short, bald, rotund man would stand in against the Brown Bomber was hilarious and frightening. Maybe the papers had been correct all along. Maybe people had been suckered by Joe Jacobs, Tony's crafty manager, a man who knew little about boxing but was a virtuoso of promotion. Maybe Jacobs, fanning the air in front of him with his cigar, cutting up sentences like flower stems, had conned them all. Maybe it was all a joke, because Galento looked like a guy fifty different men in the arena could knock out.

GALENTO pretended to skip rope, warming his body, and he, too, rose on his toes to test the floorboards. Art Donovan, the referee both camps had selected after little debate, stood in the middle of the ring dressed in a white shirt and black bowtie, dark trousers, waiting for the ring announcer, Harry Ballow, to finish the introductions. Donovan, a trim, tidy man, had officiated fights with both men before, and he gave them instructions quickly, letting them tap gloves and return to their corners. It was time to start.

Around the stadium, everyone stood. No one expected the fight to last more than a few minutes; they had paid to see the slaughter and wanted a good look at it.

As the din in Yankee Stadium rose, a southerly breeze moved the pennants on the stadium walls, and smoke from thousands of cigarettes drifted over the ring, covering it in a haze and warmth that seemed nearly inviting. The highest reaches of the stadium rested in darkness. Herring gulls occasionally lifted into flight, their beaks crossed by a fragment of pretzel or hot dog. Vendors hurried through the crowd, aware the fight might end quickly.

The seconds removed the stools. Then the timer rang the bell.

2

A PROFESSIONAL BOXER'S hand moves at a velocity of forty-six feet per second. A one-and-a-half pound fist, small for a heavyweight boxer, delivers 2,800 newtons. One newton is equal to the force exerted by the weight of a falling apple, so the gloved fist of a boxer contains the force of a pickup load of apples — sufficient energy to burst a concrete slab one and a half inches thick. For maximum impact, the punch should land at 80 percent extension, and the desired termination point should be somewhere in the opponent's mid-skull. Fortunately, bone can withstand forty times more force than concrete, and a cylindrical bone less than an inch in diameter and 2⅓ inches long can survive more than 25,000 newtons. Hands can withstand even more than that, because tendon, skin, blood, and gristle absorb some of the impact. A hand, by rough calculation, absorbs 2,000 times as much force as concrete before breaking. To accommodate such blunt power, the brain must absorb the impact in its jelly sac.

IN 1939, at the time of the Louis–Galento fight, the New York Athletic Commission permitted heavyweight boxers twelve feet of soft bandage and ten feet of one-and-a-half-inch tape with which to bind their hands. Customarily, a fighter's manager supervised the taping of his opponent's hands to ensure the hand held nothing but fingers and skin. Enclosing a metal bar in the tape, or even painting the wrap with plaster of paris, turned the fist into a cudgel. Taping a boxer's hands did nothing to protect the face or brain of either boxer. Tape guarded a man's hands. Tape kept the hands cupped like commas when they weren't curled into fists and made it possible to hit with full force over and over again.

A LOW BLOW delivers to the balls a sizable portion of the twenty-eight hundred newtons a heavyweight's hand manufactures in its arc to the scrotum. The wide athletic cup, the thick belt, can't entirely deflect that much energy. The balls crush and flatten before restoring themselves to the proper shape. Men vomit from the pain.

A CONTUSION or black eye from a blow forces bleeding into the eyelids. Deep scrapes and cuts of the cornea, usually caused by the opponent's hand pad or thumb, often resulted in the need for surgery to repair a detached retina. Likewise, a blowout fracture, the shattering of the bony structure around the eye, or a depressed cheekbone, require restorative surgery.

The pressure of a fist against an exposed ear often ruptures an eardrum. A blow to the ear also causes bleeding in the outer ear. If not drained by a physician, the blood usually forms a hard mass, creating a boxer's most storied feature: the cauliflower ear.

TO MAKE their faces coarser, more resistant to cuts, the boxers of the 1930s soaked their faces in pickle brine. In 1881's *The History of the Prize Ring*, a book perhaps wrongly attributed to William Dean Howells, John L. Sullivan's training regimen is described. In addition to walking ten miles in the morning and hitting a football suspended from a ceiling three times a day, Sullivan was sponged down with sea water to increase his skin's resistance to tears. Weak skin turns sparring dangerous, cancels fights due to small cuts, and earmarks a pugilist as a bad investment for a big bout, because blood, even at a prizefight, makes customers edgy. Whether a fighter is hurt by the punches hardly matters. A boxer who bleeds readily gains a reputation as a "tomato can," and must battle the failing of his own skin even as he fights his opponents.

IN THE CORNER, "cut men" of the 1930s employed the edge of a quarter to pop welts, gathering the ooze of blood and pus into a wet sponge. Seconds fanned their boxers, standing above them with wicker paddles to scramble the air. Small spade-shaped irons were kept in ice and pressed onto fighters' skin to freeze the blood and muck beneath a sharp swelling.

A BLOW to the solar plexus, the nerve center of the abdomen, may short-circuit the system and bring about a knockout. The liver is under the rib cage and a blow to the right ribs can tear its surface. The soft spleen is on the left side and is also prone to injury from a sharp striking blow, especially an uppercut to the left ribs.

A KNOCKOUT (KO) victory is declared when one participant is unable to rise from the canvas within a specified period of time. A referee can also declare a technical knockout (TKO) in cases where a participant is sufficiently injured, unbalanced, or confused to be unable to continue the fight. A TKO is a nod to civility and the attempt to license what is otherwise barbarous, but it is satisfactory to no one. It permits the beaten boxer to believe he might have rallied and returned to action; fans grouse about not seeing the final blow, the stunning climax they hoped for. For the referee, a TKO is a delicate balance because the consequence of an instant decision can either cost a man his life or end a bout prematurely.

* * *

TWO TON TONY FOUGHT without a mouth guard, like most fighters of his day, until later in his career. In 1929 against Jack Shaw, a tough heavyweight from Jersey, he caught an uppercut and bit his tongue in half. His mouth pulsed with blood, but he continued to fight, spitting copious amounts of red into the bucket between rounds. He beat Shaw on points but could not open his mouth to speak. At a nearby hospital Dr. Max Stern, a sports doctor who had worked on Mickey Walker, Young Stribling, Gene Tunney, and Primo Carnera, sewed Tony's tongue together with twenty-five stitches. He ordered Tony to rest in bed and to take several days of complete rest. An hour later, Tony went missing. He had disappeared when a nurse had been called away to another room, and Stern sent an orderly to the local taverns to see if they could find the patient. The orderly reported back that Tony had indeed wended his way to a pub and could be found sitting at the bar, a pint of beer in front of him. Dr. Stern followed the orderly and demanded Tony hold his tongue out for inspection. As Stern had suspected, the stitches had loosened. He ordered Tony back to the hospital, but Tony said no. "I ain't taking the count again, Doc. Gimme a glass of beer and you can go to work on me right here."

"You're crazy," the doctor warned him. "This will be a very painful operation."

"Aw, nuts," Tony said. "Don't give me that stuff. You go ahead."

Tony sat without a murmur while Stern removed the bulging stitches and replaced them with new ones. Dr. Stern, a man accustomed to the extreme pain thresholds of boxers, claimed he had never seen a display to equal it.

BEFORE THE 1920S a downed boxer was awarded no moment to rise to his feet and collect his wits. The boxer who knocked his opponent to the canvas hovered over him, blocked only by the temporary obstruction posed by the referee, ready for the instant his fallen adversary gained his wobbly stance. Immediately — sometimes pushing the ref to the side with his free hand — the advantaged boxer rushed forward, hitting his rising opponent in the chin like a man finishing the downward stroke of a saw cut. In many instances, the fallen boxer resumed his knee, the only means to get a timeout. Then the process repeated; no rule prevented a round from having a dozen knockdowns. The referee, who carried on his shoulders the fans' feverish interest, rarely interceded.

A CONCUSSION occurs when the brain is jarred against the skull with sufficient force to cause temporary loss of function in the higher centers of the brain. The injured person may remain conscious or may lose consciousness briefly, and is disoriented for some minutes after the blow. Symptoms of concussion include headache, disorientation, confusion, vacant stare or confused expression, incoherent or incomprehensible speech, lack of coordination or weakness, amnesia for the events immediately preceding the blow, nausea or vomiting, double vision, and ringing in the ears. These symptoms may last from several minutes to several hours. More severe or longer-lasting symptoms may indicate more severe brain injury.

According to the Centers for Disease Control and Prevention, approximately three hundred thousand people sustain mild to moderate sports-related brain injuries each year, most of them young men between the ages of sixteen and twenty-five. While concussion usually resolves on its own without lasting effect, it can set the stage for a much more serious condition. "Second impact syndrome" occurs when a person with a concussion, even a very mild one, suffers a second blow before fully recovering from the first. The brain swelling and increased intracranial pressure can be fatal. Second impact syndrome wasn't officially described until 1984, but boxers, trainers, and referees have known about it from their first fights.

YEARS AFTER his career was over, when checking into a motel, Joe Louis routinely buttered the ceiling with mayonnaise to keep out poisonous gases, and often built a cardboard tent atop his bed to reflect anything that might have bypassed the mayonnaise. He stuffed the vents of air-conditioners with paper wads and tucked towels under the hallway door. He believed people, government agents and the Mafia, pursued him. Whenever he traveled, he changed itineraries several times to shake off his pursuers. On May 1, 1970, the Denver sheriff's office took Louis from his home and delivered him to the Colorado Psychiatric Hospital. His third wife, Martha, had executed the order. Louis demanded to talk to the White House, to President Nixon specifically. Told he could not speak to Nixon, merely an aide, he called the *Denver Post* and the *Rocky Mountain News.* "I want everyone to know what you are doing to me," he declared. He remained three months in the hospital.

Medication eventually reversed many of the symptoms, but he remained lost, a man whose great purpose in life was over by the time he entered middle age. In addition to his other mental symptoms, it is likely he suffered from *pugilistica dementia,* or punch-drunkenness, a condition created by minute brain hemorrhages that lead to small areas of scarring. The condition is marked by slowness of speech, blurred vision, memory loss, and the boxer's shuffling gait.

3

TWO TON TONY GALENTO did not run across the ring at the bell, nor did he tackle Joe Louis as some prognosticators had promised. Sweat dripped from his forehead and arms, and the apron of his shorts had already darkened with perspiration as he crossed the ring. His black boxing shoes pegged him to the canvas, providing a contrast that made his white skin stand out from the tent color of the flooring. Referee Art Donovan backed away, abdicating, in his movement, responsibility over what must occur. Galento continued forward like a man wading a stream, knowing he must eventually strike deeper water. The heads of people at ring-side jerked to center, their eyes greedy for the moment of joining. Their faces, in the old photos, show eagerness, a cruel anticipation, and a desire to see the collision. Mixed in their expressions is a sly shame that they participated in this, and had carried the combatants forward by the price of their admissions.

BEETLE-BROWED, nearly bald, with a head that rode his collarbones like a bowling ball returning on the rails, Two Ton Tony Galento resembled, according to *Collier* magazine writer Jack Miley, "a taxi driving away with its top down." He appeared nearly square, his legs two broomsticks jammed into a vertical hay bale. He affected checked suits, a sidecar motorcycle, and a dented bowler. His thick-lipped mouth, partially open as if to persuade flies to visit, looked more comfortable turned around the boiling stem of a cigar. Along with Edward G. Robinson, he was the model for Froggy in the Courageous Cat cartoon show, a caricature of good-humored criminality, a fellow who could say "yuse guys" and make it sound as though you had joined something. Reporters from across the country came to interview him and they seldom departed disappointed at the result. To amuse them — and to startle unknowing mugs who didn't hear his approach — he developed a Tarzan yodel, a cry so loud it invariably caused those who heard it to reach for their ears. Galento liked the call so much he turned it into part of his training routine: Before entering a sparring session he howled like Johnny Weissmuller, the popular actor and Olympic athlete who played the Ape Man in four *Tarzan* epics in the 1930s' cinema. On one occasion, when Boxing Commissioner General John Phelan visited, Tony climbed in the general's car and kept performing his Tarzan yell until Phelan forcibly escaped.

Tony enjoyed being called The Ape Man, and in 1938 at the Hotel Astor's Saints & Sinners Club banquet he agreed to fight Gargantua the Great, then on exhibit at the Ringling Brothers Circus at Madison Square Garden. He had been set up by former heavyweight champ Gene Tunney, who had written an article for a local paper about the Ape vs. Human contest.

> We have been hearing much about what an Ape really would do to a human prizefighter. I stand ready to close such a match. I would select Tony Galento, our guest of honor, to fight him. If Galento can't knock out Gargantua, the Ape, then I'll forever hold my peace as well as my mouth.

Tunney proposed the match only half in jest. The notion of a missing link, of a humanoid creature half beast, half human, intrigued the American public. Tony, according to many writers of the day, represented a throwback to an earlier human ancestor. Abe Green, New Jersey State Boxing Commissioner, described Galento as one "who has a robust body, a stout chin, gameness and a punch . . . his heart pumped pure fighting blood." Both men commented on Galento's eating habits: three chickens, as many vegetables as could feed a family of five, milk, dessert, and occasionally up to fifty glasses of beer.

UNKNOWN TO anyone in the crowd but promoter Mike Jacobs, a man who shared a last name with Galento's manager, but was not related, NBC had wanted to televise the bout from Madison Square Garden. With a technology called the tele-radio, or the iconoscope, the original television contract was to be a "courtesy arrangement," with no fees passing either way. Television existed as an experimental project. The first two broadcasts — a baseball game between Columbia and Princeton, and a prizefight between Max Baer and Lou Nova — had provided a taste of what television might bring to sports. NBC hoped that the boxing broadcasts might help sell a few televisions. But in negotiating the deal for the Baer–Nova pairing in Madison Square Garden, Jacobs had begun to conceive of an idea. If television could truly capture the excitement of a major bout, only an avid fan would bother to attend the arena. How much better, he thought, to show the fight on television in various theaters, then charge individuals to enter and watch. By doing so he would reach thousands more than the average stadium could hold, increasing revenues exponentially. He had hit upon the notion of closed-circuit fight broadcasts, though he lacked the vocabulary, and the understanding of the burgeoning technology, to capitalize on it.

For now, though, such programs remained a curiosity. Nothing could replace the sight of two heavyweights moving toward each other in the first round of a championship defense. To be at the event, to hold a ticket, made a fan stand apart from his fellow citizens. Fans opened their mouths, inhaling.

A LARGE PORTION of the nation pulled for Galento, for an underdog it understood somewhere in its gut, for a clown and a man who made them laugh, who might, with superb luck, redeem their own foolish lives by giving everything in one sublime moment. He was Falstaff, robust, bawdy, a failed knight known for his dubious self-assurance and humorous rascality. No one would ever call his ring craft polished. He brawled rather than boxed. At the bell of each round he bellowed and rushed his opponent, diving forward into the fight, haymakers and roundhouses his punches of choice. He absorbed great punishment, yet he always moved forward, ceaseless, his determination marked in his movement, in his capacity to endure pain. Frequently cut and wiping away blood, he did not retreat. No one had knocked him out. No one had even knocked him off his feet. He fought by will primarily and relied on a single crushing punch that could save the day in even the most lopsided loss. One could not root against him any more than one could root against oneself.

They did not hate Joe Louis, not all of them, at any rate, but the Brown Bomber exhibited grace in a thousand ways they could not hope to replicate. They did not root for Tony Galento to win, necessarily, but to fight with dignity, to be better than he had a right to be. And they rooted for an explosion, a bestial collision between Galento and Louis. Nothing about the fight promised beauty, or even the athletic grace of a masterful boxer picking apart his foe. Galento was a cherry bomb dropped into a water pipe. People watched with joy and a readiness to wince at what might occur.

* * *

TONY CAME to scratch first, crossing the middle of the ring, his body crouched, his hands at the sides of his head as if prepared to lock his thumbs in his ears like a pretend bull. His mouth, never closed during the fight, sagged open to reveal his mouth guard. His fleshy lips pushed forward to take air, a camel's lips bent around thorns. Joe Louis, rising to meet him, extended his left and kept it out, his reach creating a string that established his arc around his opponent. For a moment they merely stood in front of each other. Then Tony, jumping and slashing with his left, swatted twice, his eagerness throwing him off balance. Louis danced to the side and away, slipping the first attack and taking an instant to regroup. His height established a slight awkwardness, because to punch at Tony made him shove down, like a man stuffing a dresser drawer too full. Neither man landed anything worthwhile. They resumed positions in front of one another. Twenty seconds of the fight was over.

THE CROWD REACTED to the opening exchange, but not overzealously. Politicians, important officials, sports and entertainment celebrities watched from ten feet away, their eyes at shin level to the fighters, the beauty and intimacy of the boxers' exchanges brilliant and pleasing and frightening. These were men who knew fights and, like men who frequent sex shows and can no longer be easily titillated, they talked as they watched, smoked, relaxed, and felt the pleasure of sitting front row at an event discussed and debated for weeks and months. It did not do to appear too avid; to be a fan, yes, but to observe the fighters with undue passion suggested a lack of a broad appreciation of past fights. To gain their full attention, the bout must rise above the average exchange. These men, well known and followed by the press, waited to be shown. And at that moment, they watched as Two Ton Tony leaped forward and connected with a left hook that had half his life behind it.

THINK OF A round, hard baseball connecting with the fibrous heart of an ash bat. Think of the ball's flesh sinking into itself for the barest instant, the bat yielding, the fibers in the wood, the same fibers that kept the tree erect in winds for twenty or thirty years, pulling apart and then returning the force of the ball. Think of the solid sweetness, the ultimate surprise of the forces exchanging and releasing, the simplicity of it after all, and the long arc of the ball speeding away. Think of Galento's ham-sized fist, 12½ inches around, and the force traveling up his arm, the shoulder spreading and gaping with muscle, the wiggle of his belly as the power and energy transferred itself to his body, and the thrust of Louis's head going away from the fist as fast as his muscles allowed. Think of a strand of saliva escaping from Louis's mouth, the silver glimmer of it as it reflected cigarette smoke and lights and camera flashes, its liquid pull falling to the canvas, his mouthpiece, for the period of one breath, coming loose in his mouth and readjusting to his bite as the pain and surprise of the punch registered in his brain.

* * *

JOE LOUIS staggered backward. The crowd ignited. *Did you see that?* passed like a great hiss around the forty-thousand spectators. People reached for one another, grabbing the nearest arm, eyes still on the ring. After all the ballyhoo, all the gaudy pre-fight promotion, Tony Galento had landed a full-bore left hook on the tip of Joe Louis's chin and driven the champion to the ropes.

IF THE PUNCH had landed five years before for Galento — before a nearly fatal case of pneumonia that required three blood transfusions the previous year, before the hundreds of punches received and given, before the toll of food and drink had done its damage — it might have finished Louis. If the punch had landed five years later for Louis, if he had not been in his prime, in superb physical condition, the punch may have proven too much. But a fight is often an X for two men crossing in different directions, and the punch that staggered Louis was merely the rivet joining a pair of scissor blades.

LOUIS WAS VISIBLY stunned. His knees hinged. The New Jersey fans pounded each other, and they screamed when Tony followed up with a right cross, hacking down at the champion as if letting his hand fall from a subway strap. But Louis, relying on training, had his gloves up and the punch glanced off harmlessly. In his hurry to follow up the massive left, Galento scattered his power. Louis, uncurled by the punch, slowly gained his posture again, his slight bend forward. He rubbed his shoulders on the top rope, flexed, and pushed away. He moved left, away from Galento's heavy hand, and maneuvered back to the center of the ring. His head rang. His feet slowly found the floor properly again. He fended off punches, landed two, landed another, moved.

The round continued. Galento punched furiously, but Louis had his stride now, his body finally warm. Louis's magnificent form — the sweet, smooth gears of his shoulders and arms — shot out punches in direct lines at Galento's face. He wasted no motion. One writer described his jab as a light bulb bursting on your face. The Bomber's seconds shouted for him to wake up, to move, and he did. He backpedaled and circled to his left, letting Tony frog-hop after him. Louis's punches began to jar Galento's head back onto his shoulders, but Tony continued forward, lumbering and lurching to get closer. As a short man with a limited reach, Galento accepted the bargain of bruising jabs to get the position he needed.

Louis hit Galento freely, chucking his head back and taking the vertical line out of his opponent's body. Years later, toy manufacturers would make plastic action figures, hulking, brutish men whose arms hang beside their bodies, their foreheads primitive and forward-thrusting. Galento resembled such toys, a galumphing troglodyte whose purpose on earth smoked in his narrow brain as impulses to break, bruise, and crunch. No matter that of the two boxers Galento had claims to being the more verbally adroit, the greater showman. It was

Two Ton Tony Galento, with his cigar-smoking, jackhammer-tongued manager, Joe Jacobs, who appeared at the Stork Club in tails and top hats and was introduced to Noel Coward. Two sportswriters along for the ride — John Carmichael and Caswell Adams — reported the following exchange.

> "Who's he?" Galento asked about Coward.
> "The British playwright," he was told.
> "Oh," Tony said, "Hiya, pally, in-deedy."

As they made their way across the room, the reporters introduced him to Orson Welles, who had recently terrorized the country with his radio broadcast of *The War of the Worlds*. "So you're the guy with dem Martians, eh? I kin knock dem all out!"

Tony didn't much like the Stork Club either. "It's a swell joint," he said, "but look at how empty it is." He left the nightclub main floor in order to go upstairs and play craps with the musicians.

Now Louis, who had been prevented as a black man from speaking, jibbing, teasing for fear of losing favor with the boxing matchmakers, for fear of alienating the white money behind the championship belt, used his exquisite body to express himself, while Galento, glib and hilarious, caught the battering. Tony leaped and burbled; Louis, upright and stoic, spoke with his hands.

AT SOME POINT a bout belongs only to the fighters inside the ring, and for a moment, Louis and

Galento entered that phase. The crowd no longer mattered; the fuss and bother of getting to the ring had at last ended. Finally, even after Galento's big punch, they stood toe to toe, trading punches and testing each other's resolve. All the sparring, the rope skipping, the jogging, shrank to a small, silent point where the two men, not as names in the newspapers, but as human beings, looked at the shape and angle of one another's faces, saw the other's chest, his arm hair, his bulging ear. They observed the imperfection of the other, and hoped to see signs of weakness there. Perhaps in some part of their memories each recalled another opponent who reminded him of the man in front of him now.

Louis, naturally, had to face white men as a rule, so the pale luminescence under the lights must have seemed not in the least unusual. For Galento, Louis may have appeared more exotic. Galento had fought black men before and fared poorly against them. He feared them as a curse on his career, their gliding skills antithetical to his bludgeoning technique. He had once nearly refused a proposed match at ringside when he stepped through the ropes and found an Irish name attached to a black man. Now he faced Louis, a light-skinned black man, but a man whose hair appeared different from his own, whose lips, and eyes, and brow ridge did not mirror his own. Galento embraced the racist stereotypes of his day, and to him, certainly, Louis appeared a nigger, a datsoon, a darkie. But in that instant when the fight became theirs, Louis could at last insist on his humanity, on his equality, and as they blocked and traded punches, Galento felt forced to concede that much. It occurred to him, and perhaps to Louis, that despite their differences they had more in common, by virtue of their pairing in the ring, than most men share in a lifetime. Who else could they speak to about this night when it finished? Who would know it as they did? They turned and moved and reflected each other, their arms hacking viciously at one another's defenses as if trying to climb inside the other man's ribs.

THE BELL sounded to end round one as both men stood in the center of the ring. Referee Donovan stepped in and signaled the end, his white shirt already dotted with sweat and flecks of blood. Tony instantly dropped his arms and opened his mouth. Whether he spoke was impossible to tell in the crowd noise, but Louis turned away, immediately assuming his spot on his corner stool. Tony walked leisurely back to his handlers. Joe Jacobs and Jimmy Frain, and Whitey Bimstein — a longtime trainer at Stillman's Gym who was described by A. J. Liebling as "a small, bald man with side-hair the color of an Easter chick" — flamed up from their station and ringed around him. They could barely contain themselves. Every fight judge and expert in attendance awarded the first round to Galento. In Louis's six title defenses, three of the contenders survived less than two minutes. Galento had landed the only telling blow so far. It was possible he had Louis's number; stranger things had happened. Someday, if Louis remained in the ring long enough, he would lose. That was a boxing certainty. And no one would know how it would happen until it did.

Then it would appear plain and inevitable. Until then, everything existed as a promise, and Galento had as much claim as anyone.

AROUND RADIOS across the country, people turned and called to others nearby who had ignored the fight or thought it would be lopsided, and informed them that Galento had given a good accounting. Forty million fans, their ears caught by the excitement in the radio announcer's voice, called to friends and told them they really had to listen to this. Something had occurred. Louis was losing. Galento had buckled the champ's knees. The greatest upset of all time, maybe. That fat guy was winning, the one who smoked cigars and said he would moida da bum. The bartender. That guy. The crowd at the stadium could not dream of taking a seat. The horses outside the ballpark dozed, the mounted police stationed on them receiving reports from men who hurried in and out of the stadium, from the radios that carried the fight into the streets, until the noise of the contest proved inescapable, even if escape had been desired.

A few people remembered the morning column written by John Kieran in the *New York Times*. Speculating on the fight and the lowered betting odds, he wrote

> In short, what they (the fans and gamblers) viewed as an uproarious farce at long range they viewed as a serious fight as the hour of combat drew near. Now, even the most timid person must know that his chances of being struck by lightning are slim. He can

> be shown the figures on the total population of this country and the number of persons struck by lightning in the course of the year. It would be ridiculous to think that he was running much risk according to those figures. He snaps his fingers boldly at the sky.
>
> Then it clouds up. The air is sultry. Thunder is heard in the distance. A lightning storm is coming over. The wind rises with an ominous swish. The rain comes down in buckets. And the timid gent is out in the storm!
>
> Ah! Now he views his chance of being struck by lightning in a very different light. Crack! Boom! Never mind the figures now. All he knows is he might be hit. That's the thing that grips his mind at the moment.

Suddenly, after the thudding first round, the fight did not appear so preposterous. What had been a sure thing moments before now appeared a coin toss. Galento had won the first round.

4

As immigrants from El Barona, Italy, the Galentos joined a massive wave of Italians seeking better circumstances in Latin America and the United States. Fleeing earthquake, a tidal wave, and the spread of phylloxera, a disease that killed grape vines, 4.5 million Italian citizens came to American shores before and after the turn of the twentieth century. By 1914 one out of every twenty Italians in Italy had been to America at least once, according to Thomas Hauser and Stephen Brunt in *The Italian Stallions.* A cholera epidemic that killed fifty-five thousand people pushed the immigration faster, increasing it until Benito Mussolini and the Fascists took power in 1924 and closed the exit doors.

The Italians, like the Irish, missed homesteading opportunities open to the Swedes and Dutch and Germans who had arrived earlier and had pushed west immediately.

Instead, they settled in urban areas, populating the infamous Lower East Side in Manhattan, their language and culture strange to the more established immigrant groups. They faced bigotry and violence; American "nativists" scolded them and called for them to return to Italy. Stuffed into tenements run by pirate landlords, without recourse to government officials or means of protest, the immigrants suffered from relentless cold in winter, and hen-sized rats in summer. They called the rats *zoccolas,* Italian slang for whores, and they knew to avoid where rats ran pressed to the thresholds made from the joint of building facades and street pavement.

As Catholics, Italians considered reproduction a religious obligation, and so the tenements filled to overflowing. Jake LaMotta in *Raging Bull,* his famous account of the time, speaks of the stench found there:

> What I remember about the tenement as much as anything is the smell. It's impossible to describe the smell of a tenement to someone who's never lived in one. You can't just put your head in the door and sniff. You have to live there, day and night, summer and winter, so the smell gets a chance to sink into your soul. There's all that dirt that the super never really manages to get clean even on the days when he does an hour's work, and this dirt has a smell, gray and dry, and, after you smelled it long enough, suffocating. And diapers. The slobs who live in tenements are always having kids, and naturally they don't have the money for any diaper service, so the old lady is

always boiling diapers on the back of the stove and after a while the smell gets into the walls.

But life in the Italian section of Newark and the Oranges had its marvelous compensations, according to Michael Immerso, author of *Newark's Little Italy.* Entire families slept out on fire escapes during the hottest nights, and during late summer the neighborhood smelled of bubbling tomato sauce, garlic, and onions. In the same season the men piled rubbery mounds of ripe grapes at curbside, and the serious business of wine making, with its friendly rivalry, consumed the populations of city blocks. Peddlers passed by with rich, repetitive appeals, the rag man, *U stracciare,* singing, "Any rags, any bones, any bottles today?" And the Jewish peddler known as Jack the Bean Stalk, who sold pots and pans, called the customers by name; the knife and scissors man, who carried a grinding stone on his shoulder, made the instruments cling to rhythm as they took an edge. *U pizzaiole,* the pizza peddler, wore a white hat and a baker's apron, and on his shoulder he balanced a copper tray stacked with individual pizzas covered by a lid to keep them warm. The peddler of fancy meats, who sold tripe, liver, lungs, and hearts, stood at curbside and waited while cooking women lowered baskets with a few cents in the bottom, then, after shouted negotiations, sliced off the requisite amount and sent it bouncing back up the side of the building. Sometimes, too, the women of the building skipped the ice man's delivery and went instead to the local market, where they purchased ice and carried it back on their heads, the lines of melt making bright flashes on their foreheads. They carried their unbaked bread to the bakery, too, and returned, after paying a small fee for the use of the ovens, with the baked bread on their heads.

The women, masters of *malocchio*, the evil eye, used spells to change the tides to their liking. They put headaches on loud neighbors, sank bellyaches in children, caused businesses to rupture. In remedy a wise neighbor woman might put a drop of oil into a dish, place her hand on the forehead of the sufferer, and trace the sign of the cross to draw out the pain. When she began to moan and yawn, the bubble of oil in the dish might break, relieving the sufferer of all pain.

The women often used leaf lard rather than cooking oil, heating the lard in a frying pan, squeezing it dry until only brittle bits remained. They baked the bits in ciccoli bread. Using a *gittara*, a board fitted with strings like a zither, women prepared homemade noodles, and sometimes curled the pasta with an iron needle. By the end of the 1930s, in answer to demand, Brooklyn and Queens had eight major macaroni plants in operation.

When families could not pay their electric bill, or when they missed a rent, they often took their problem to the parish priest, who more often than not found a way to pay the debt. Ritchie the Boot Boiardo, the most powerful man in Newark's Italian First Ward, frequently paid bills for families without their knowledge, or sent a truckload of coal or wood to a needy widow. But Ritchie the Boot was most famous for paying his associates with barrels of silver dollars, his trademark. A friend and associate of Al Capone's, for years he carried on a feud with Longey Zwillman, a Jewish Newark boss, adding an element of rivalry that made life in the streets dangerously sweet.

ONE HUNDRED THOUSAND immigrants entered New York during the 1930s, changing forever the face and sense of the city. Equally important, the sons and daughters of the immigrants who had arrived at the turn of the century finally had reached maturity. America could no longer pretend to be a nation of WASPs. The rise of ethnic identity changed every field it touched. Not until the conclusion of World War II would the country bend — however unsuccessfully — toward a common identity.

In addition, the population had been seared by the Depression. Following the stock market crash of 1929, poverty, and ethnic schism, deepened. Suicide rates grew by 30 percent between 1929 and 1930. The repeal of Prohibition in 1933, though welcomed by many, increased the level of alcoholism around the nation.

In New York one night in 1930, four hundred thousand people requested lodging. In January, 1931, eighty-five thousand people waited for meals on a single day. By 1932 only 47.6 percent of Italian households had an adult wage earner. Forty percent of blacks had no jobs. Many black women lined up each morning in "slave markets" where white women from the richer districts would hire them for cleaning at twenty-five cents an hour. When Cardinal Spellman took over the New York diocese in 1939, the church stood twenty-eight million dollars in debt.

Rarely has a man been better suited to a job than the mayor of New York at that period — Fiorello LaGuardia. His father, an Italian Protestant, married a Jewish woman. LaGuardia himself was Episcopalian. As a young man he worked in Budapest with Hungarians seeking immigration, acted as a translator at Ellis Island, and represented East Harlem in Congress. He spoke German, Croatian, Italian, and a smattering of several other languages. Called an anti-Semite once during a campaign, he issued a challenge to his attacker to have a debate, stipulating only that the debate be held in Yiddish — another language in which he was fluent.

LaGuardia loved New York and went everywhere. He followed fire trucks, visited exhibitions, attended fairs. Landing in Newark Airport, he refused to deplane because his ticket, he pointed out, said New York. "Newark is Newark," he argued, "and New York is New York. Don't confuse the two." Not long afterward, New York had its own airport. When the 1939 World's Fair broke ground, LaGuardia posed running a steam shovel.

Maybe no country in the world has ever boasted a city more diverse than New York in the 1930s. Living side by side, often in squalor, immigrants, and the sons and daughters of immigrants, fought for space. Languages mixed; cultures collided. The city divided into zones or neighborhoods, each holding a core of an ethnic group. Blacks, leaving deplorable conditions in the south, moved north and found little waiting for them. Jewish immigrants clustered around Washington Heights, their lives revolving around a few scattered synagogues. The Irish held Hell's Kitchen, the Italians Little Italy.

* * *

LIKE MANY boys of the period, Tony Galento had been bitten by the drama of the Jack Dempsey v. George Carpentier fight, broadcast to a national audience in 1922. The fight, held in a green wood stadium built by Tex Rickard, the nation's top fight promoter, at Boyles Thirty Acres in Jersey City, gave proof to the boys of Orange that a local contest could be important around the world. Dempsey, famous for defeating Jess Willard, the fighter who in his day had beaten the golden-toothed Jack Johnson, cracked two of Willard's ribs and fractured the large man's jaw in less than three rounds in Toledo, Ohio. Dempsey fought with rage. Jack Sharkey said after a Dempsey bout that, "You come out of a fight full of welts and bruises and every bone aching."

The Dempsey–Carpentier fight raised the first million-dollar purse and provided, in its pairing of a foreigner against an American, an early model for the Louis–Schmeling fight. Prizefighting could be international, with the honor of an athlete's country riding on the outcome. Like Schmeling, the Frenchman Carpentier, a light-heavyweight, relied on style and evasiveness, while Dempsey embodied brute American force. Even the names — Dempsey the Manassa Mauler, Carpentier the Orchid Man — underscored the contrast. The fact that Carpentier — a French war hero — was pitted against Dempsey, a suspected "slacker" who had deliberately stayed out of World War I, added contrast and intrigue to the bout. The result, a glorious win by Dempsey, turned him into an object of post–World War I adulation greater than Babe Ruth.

* * *

DURING GALENTO'S childhood boxing permeated every corner of New York City and the surrounding area. With twenty-two fight clubs in the city boroughs, and each club carrying its local tough on its shoulders, people, especially men, did not see boxing as existing apart from their everyday lives. Routinely they made arrangements to meet at the Laurel Garden, or the Newark Armory, fighting venues that promised interesting cards several times a week. Sports, except as an experiment, did not exist on television. Nothing, except family commitment, drew them home and so they met in groups, glad to be relieved for the night of familial duties.

To satisfy the customer demand, boxers fought two or three times a month; as amateurs, they boxed even more frequently. Fighters arrived on foot, came from other jobs, went to work the next morning. They trained in YMCAs, or in barrooms, or in a makeshift garage. They boxed as cousins, uncles, brothers-in-law, the family putting forward its toughest kid to prove the house honor. The excitement of it, the bloodiness, added to the potential tragedy or glory. Victory vindicated the lowered state of the boxer. He might not be rich, or educated, but, *argumentum ad lazarum,* his poverty combined with his success in the ring produced a belief that he could be more virtuous, more stouthearted, as a result. Each fighter could be a Horatio Alger, a rags-to-riches tale that the American public loved.

Newspapers ran daily boxing columns, sizing up matches, giving a preview of the night's card. Writers — Damon

Runyon, Grantland Rice, Ring Lardner, Heywood Broun, H. L. Mencken, and George Bernard Shaw all covered boxing at times — churned out thousands of columns reviewing fights and suggesting matches. *The Star-Ledger,* Galento's hometown paper, produced enormous sports-page sketches of boxers, the outsized caricatures focusing on a known element of the fighter's countenance or peculiarities in the ring. Galento, naturally, appeared as an overgrown child, a wiggly rounded creature blunted with neoteny. Pugs were social sidecars; the most successful could travel in better circles, circulating to the top of the social ladder. Like gangsters, boxers brought a dangerous glimmer to any society event. They could be counted on to misbehave, to act absurdly, but that was also their charm.

Such success, though, lingered a long way from the Laurel Garden and Newark Armory. Most boxers came and went, winning or losing, then retired. They joined the rows of men surrounding the latest boxers, the newest sensation, the kid who was all heart and a great right cross. The one from down the street. That kid, the one from over the barber shop.

FIGHTS BROUGHT the most heat, and the largest crowd, when one neighborhood stood against a nearby neighborhood; ethnic rivalry resulted as a natural byproduct. Fighters and their entourages routinely employed slurs against their opponents. Stereotypes — the Jew, the Wop, the Colored — went virtually unchallenged. Newspapers referred to Italian ballplayers as "walloping wops" or "dashing dagos." In a 1936 *Collier's Weekly* a sportswriter said about the new Yankee centerfielder, "He says you pronounce it Dee-Mah-gee-o. That's a very tough name to pronounce and also tough to spell. DiMaggio sounds like something you put on a steak."

A victory for a representative of any ethnic group became a victory for an entire ethnic population, and became, *ipso facto,* proof of the loser's ethnic inferiority. To win an important match, or to conquer an opposing hero, turned a young man into an instant neighborhood celebrity. For a defiant, scrappy young man, especially one raised with the privation typical of immigrant life, stepping off the street and into the ring seemed a natural, nearly inevitable, transition.

With his friend Jimmie Frain, ten-year-old Tony Galento built a makeshift gymnasium in the backyard of his modest Orange home on Day Street. He weight-lifted, trained on a crazy bag — a bag suspended between ceiling and floor on an elasticized rope — and filled sacks with sand for punching bags. With Jimmy casting sacks at him, Tony practiced nailing an attacker in midair. The bags, as heavy as retrievers, thudded and dropped. At school, meanwhile, Tony terrorized his teachers. He fought regularly with other boys, a pudgy, indomitable figure in tweed knickerbockers over red woolen underwear, and a go-to-hell-hat. The long johns served to keep out the raw New Jersey winters and insulated him from the blocks of ice he hauled in the dimness before the morning bell. At age ten he quit school, telling his teachers that he preferred to "earn a bit." Like many boys in his neighborhood, he raised rabbits and pigeons in the backyard. In short order he bought a horse, set up his own ice wagon, and quickly began making a living. A few years later the horse died in the street, and Tony mourned the animal's passing with a long fit of crying. He erected a monument in the backyard, declaring at the time that, "The horse was as strong as I was and I had to have something built for his memory." He bought an ice truck later, but remembered the horse fondly the rest of his life.

LIKE DOZENS of icemen in Orange, his day, every day except Sunday, began at four in the morning. Typically he loaded three-foot-long cakes on end, piling the truck with two to five tons of ice. He hosed down the ice to remove sawdust, then spread a tarpaulin over the contents. Using tongs or a shoulder bag, often both, he carried ice to buildings and apartments that put 50-pound or 25-pound requests in their windows, lugging the blocks up steps to wooden iceboxes. The iceboxes, lined with zinc and insulated with sawdust or seaweed, dripped into a pan that was emptied daily. Depending on his mood, or the standing of the customer, an iceman eyed the block and hacked off more or less according to his likes, then repeated the process throughout the day, making as many as three hundred deliveries before quitting at eight. In fact, as an amateur and pro Tony often delivered ice on the way to a prizefight. For one bout he arrived late. His cornerman at the time, a buttonhole manager named Harry Pop Kinney, reprimanded him, yelling, "Where the hell have you been?" "Don't you know you're supposed to be fighting tonight?"

"Take it easy," said Tony, "I had two tons of ice to deliver on my way here. I'll be right up."

"Two tons of ice! You've got some nerve delivering ice when you should be in the ring."

From that night Tony received his most famous nickname: Two Ton Tony Galento. Sports writers assumed his nickname came from his pulchritude, and in time that meaning would gain legitimacy. But the origin of his name was in ice.

AT THE TAIL end of 1932, Tony demanded more attention from his manager at the time, Max Waxman. Waxman had just returned from a successful trip to Europe, and he wondered aloud if he needed the annoyance of training Tony. Vince Dundee, Waxman's main fighter, appeared headed toward a championship. When Tony pushed for more consideration, Waxman happily sold Galento's contract to Pete Dodd, a lifelong friend of Galento's, but a man without any experience or contacts in the boxing world. Dodd, game for an adventure, paid Waxman $750. Almost immediately it must have appeared a bum deal for Dodd. After working to sign Galento to fight Arthur DeKuh, a 6'4" country puncher, on April 11 at Dreamland Park, Newark, Dodd found himself alone at the arena the afternoon of the weigh-in. Whatever recklessness Tony had been guilty of in the past, he knew to draw the line at missing a weigh-in. Dodd, who knew Tony's haunts, sent out a posse of men to look for the fighter, but the search turned up empty. A reporter slipped the item in the afternoon paper, and Abe Simon, owner of the Newark Loew's Theater, recognized Galento as the fellow snoring through two movies. He called Dodd, and Dodd came to fetch his fighter.

The story Tony told his trainer on the way to the bout did not make Dodd happy. Earlier that day at a local bar, Tony ate fifty hot dogs on a bet. For good measure, he ate two additional dogs, then crawled into the Loew's, where he intended to digest pleasantly until weigh-in time. The food proved heavier than he expected, and he slept longer than intended, his breathing noisy as a scuba diver's. Rushed to the locker room, Tony discovered he could no longer fit into his trunks. They sliced a small slit in his waistband, tugged to make sure it wouldn't explode, then sent him into the fray.

DeKuh, annoyed at the irregularities, punched Tony around the ring for two rounds. Gradually, though, Tony began to feel less stuffed and he told Dodd he would stop the fight in the third. He charged across the ring at the bell starting the third round and caught DeKuh flush in the nose. Blood sprayed in a great halo around DeKuh's head before he crashed to the canvas. It had been, one writer said, as if someone had stepped on a water balloon — only the balloon had been filled with blood. The referee counted DeKuh out, then waved the medical team in to survey the damage. The team rushed DeKuh to Beth Israel Hospital, not realizing they had witnessed the end of another fighter's fragile career. DeKuh later became a wrestling stooge, a great pole of a man that crowds loved to see tormented, but his boxing days had effectively ended that night.

A potential heavyweight contender was discovered in "Tough Tony Galento," wrote Tony Marenghi in the *Newark Star-Eagle*. "He ought to go places in boxing if he tends to his knitting and trains and takes advice from his handlers."

IN 1935–36, Krueger Beer of Newton, New Jersey, introduced the first canned beer, the same year former alcoholic Bill Wilson and Dr. Robert H. Smith founded Alcoholics Anonymous. Americans' ambivalence about alcohol played out in movies and radio shows, where actors performed stock impersonations of inebriates, their sloshing antics a running source of humor. The repeal of Prohibition in 1933 — though six southern states, Kansas, and North Dakota remained dry — ushered in a national love of tomfoolery with booze and beer.

Tony Galento, on the advice of Joe Jacobs, his manager by then, and smelling the cultural wind himself, put a deposit on a saloon on Day Street in Orange and opened for business. If anyone had been born to be a saloon keeper, it was Two Ton Tony Galento. Jacobs, who believed fighters needed a business besides fighting, told Tony the publicity he received as a fighter would attract patrons. Tony, studying the sporting tavern set up by his former manager, Pete Dodd, saw dollar signs.

In his inimitable style, Tony found a bear and bought it so that he could put on sparring exhibitions. Nights he could be found ducking swats from a bear, his girth cinched tight by a white bar apron, a thick cigar plunked in one corner of his mouth. His model for the enterprise, he claimed, was the Boston Strong Boy, John L. Sullivan, a prizefighter who could drink as well as he boxed. While the New Jersey Boxing Commission greeted the prospect of a boxer running a bar with a nervous glance, newspaper reporters found the combination irresistible.

"Beer never hurt anyone," Tony told the reporters at the opening. "Of course, I have my limitations. I use it a little when I go into training camp."

The saloon proved such a sensation that Galento stepped temporarily out of the ring. If he could earn money simply by pulling a beer tap, boxing did not seem as attractive. But then Al Delaney, a rising star in New Jersey, caught Jacobs's attention, and he convinced Tony it would be a good match. Out of shape and chunky with beer, Galento looked like a side-railed train against the young, spry contender. He lost in six. As soon as the fight ended, Jacobs ordered Galento into serious training, telling his fighter it was pointless to schedule bouts if he could not count on him. For once in his life, Tony acceded.

Tony fought Eddie Blunt in Newark on April 6, 1936. Blunt, known for a quick, short rabbit punch, went into the bout a 5 to 1 favorite, but by the ninth round the fighters had turned the fight into a donnybrook, both of them falling to the floor and wrestling around the canvas. When the referee succeeded in breaking them apart, Galento caught Blunt with a left hook to the temple. He followed with a right hand and knocked Blunt down for a nine count. Blunt could not regroup and Galento won a decision, his name back in the papers as a potential contender.

New Jersey fight fans called for a rematch with Al Delaney and the fight was booked for May 11. Down to 220 pounds, Galento reported to the match in honest fighting shape. Inspector John Painter Donnelly of the New Jersey Boxing Commission, however, banned Joe Jacobs from the bout for his refusal to take out a license in the Garden State. Jacobs, furious, threatened to pull Galento out of the arena. Fortunately for his boxing future, Galento insisted on the fight continuing as planned, and with Jimmy Frain and Dick O'Connor in his corner, he fought to a draw with Delaney.

With or without Jacobs, fighting kept Tony in the papers. His celebrity in New Jersey paid dividends in the saloon. With Mary at the cash register and Tony behind the bar, fans lined up outside the entrance, waiting to get inside to see the New Jersey Night Stick. Tony, notoriously cheap, grabbed friends and relatives and threw them behind the bar to serve drinks. He rarely paid them, and once, according to his sister-in-law, Mildred, charged his brother Russell fifteen cents for a pack of cigarettes even though Russell fixed his brother's cars and tended bar for free. As the writer Bob Considine described it, Tony was "tighter than a rain swollen desk drawer."

Tony also gambled. In a room above the saloon, he set up a poker den where he played for high stakes, occasionally becoming so angry at a losing hand that he threw chairs through the upstairs windows, showering glass on the customers waiting outside. With a band playing downstairs, a crowd lined up along the sidewalk, a bear taking on the proprietor, and chairs occasionally falling from the second story, the Galentos' saloon gained a pleasant hint of danger.

Tony's picture appeared repeatedly in the newspaper, a beer glass cocked against his heavy lips, a white apron serving as a cummerbund for his sizeable gut, his meaty arms ended by a bar rag. His standard line, when asked how he would fare against this or that boxer, was his patented, "I'll moida da bum." He had found the fulcrum he had always wanted and he began to lift.

CHILEAN Arturo Godoy, a fighter not dissimilar to Tony, signed to fight the New Jersey Night Stick at the New York Hippodrome in April 1937. Godoy, who went on to fight Louis twice, both times giving the champion fits (and by many accounts fighting Louis to a draw in the first contest), ripped left hooks at Galento. He also rushed and mauled, a mirror of Tony's style. As *Times* columnist John Kieran reported about their pairing, the two fighters "were funny. They made it a free for all, catch as catch can, and used everything except spurs on one another." Godoy won, but the fight proved exciting enough that Joe Jacobs sent them both to Chicago to fight in the "all heavyweight" preliminary before the Braddock–Louis championship bout. The second matching turned out to be every bit as rough as the first and concluded with the same result.

Afterward, *Times* reporter Bob Considine interviewed Godoy about Galento:

> "Some fallow!" Godoy said, holding his head. "First time we fight, he so toff — roff — tuff. Four round he do every to me. He poosh, he bott, he bock-hand, he

step on foot. Donovan [the referee] step in a between us and he say 'Galento, you cud that stoff. I give fight to Godoy.' Galento keep doing, and finally I come back to corner after four round and say to Whitey Bimstein, 'what I do, what I do, with man who fights like he do?' Bimstein say, 'do.'

"Do, do. Do like Galento do. I'm very glad to hear that. Very much. So I go out and the first thing I say a bad word, and I hit him in his eye. Cut. Then I say more bad words. Terrible. And I fight like Galento do, and next round he say, when we clinch, 'why you getting mad me Godoy? I'm only kid you.' How do you like that? Some bull.

"After the fight we go to dressing room and his mad. I say 'you mad for you lose decision,' and he wants to fight again. He push me, like this, and I say, 'yeah, all right, Galento, come on . . .' But fallows come up and they say, 'don't be zap — fighting for nuthen.'

"Pretty soon we fight again in Chicago. Now I know him. I know what to do. I give roff-stoff, bing, bang — plenty toff. And when we near the finish he hug me and say 'we cud fight again in New Yersey, huh? Plenty dough New Yersey.' I say 'okay-doke we fight in New Yersey, but you have raffrey, jodges, people all for you in New Yersey. Okay-doke, you have them, just let me kick you, boom, like this, and bit you, aarrrgh, like this, and we even.' So we don't fight New Yersey. Someday I like take Galento in Chile. Hah. I would like to fight in Chile with Galento. Then he would see real ruff-stoff plenty."

Despite its brutality, the fight in Chicago held a comic edge. The referee, Dave Miller, happened to be nearly as bulky as Galento. With the boxers battling and slipping gouges at each other, Galento decided to let Miller enjoy some of the recreation. He punched the referee, staggering him for an instant. When the bell rang, the two hundred and forty pound ref sailed to Joe Jacobs' corner and said, "You're not fighting me, Mr. Galento. You're fighting that fellow over there. See, over there."

"Yes," replied Tony, "and if you annoy me in the clinches again, I'll flatten you, too. And I'm not fooling."

After the Godoy fight, Tony returned to the locker room angry and keenly disappointed. He felt he had been robbed. James Braddock, who had lost the world heavyweight title to Joe Louis earlier in the night, sat in the same locker room, slowly undressing. Tony, enraged, asked for Braddock's sympathy.

"Say," Galento said, "it was tough, wasn't it, Jim?"

"Yes, it was," Braddock mumbled.

"Yeah, that guy Miller gave Godoy the duke."

"Oh, I thought you were talking about me losing my title," said Braddock, amused at Galento's focus on himself.

Despite the loss, Galento had become a property. He made for good copy. He fought viciously, ducked no one, and did it all with a beer bottle and a cigar close by. His training practices, or lack of them, endeared him to the general population. While boxing fans could not hope to emulate the Spartan training regimes of most fighters, the average fan delighted in Tony's poolroom gymnasium. Joe

Jacobs had taken a fourth-rate fighter, a man nearly finished with boxing, and had turned him into a potential contender.

Galento had become a household name across the country, but in the Oranges and Newark he was identified and cheered wherever he went, a true celebrity. In the 1937 National Boxing Association's fourth-quarter ratings of heavyweight contenders, Galento ranked behind Buddy Baer in the number three position. He could fill a stadium now. New Jerseyans howled for a fight with Joe Louis and flooded the papers with letters comparing the two.

TONY GALENTO had the nation's interest. As a figure of fun, or as a serious contender, he appeared everywhere, irrepressible and as present as only American celebrities can be. Martin Gable, who portrayed Julius Ceaser in Orson Welles's production of the Shakespeare play, told the great director, "You're certainly getting on, Orson. You're getting almost as much publicity as Tony Galento."

Galento, on the other hand, was asked what he thought of Shakespeare. "Never hoid of him," Tony answered. "What's he, one of those foreign heavyweights? I'll moida da bum."

On July 9, 1938, four days before a roaring welcome and a parade of a half million people in Philadelphia for a scheduled bout with John Henry Lewis, a light-heavyweight noted for his smooth style and mongoose speed, the *New York Times* reported that Galento knocked out two sparring partners in three rounds at Madame Bey's training facility in

Summit, New Jersey. He floored Lew Brown with a left hook, then smashed Larry Johnson with a right hand that all but fractured the man's jaw. Al Albin, a light-heavyweight brought in to replicate Lewis's style, boxed two successful rounds with Two Ton. The *Washington Post* reported the following day that Galento was in danger of running out of sparring partners. His strength and punching power had never been more formidable.

After a twelve-round workout in Bey's outdoor ring four days before the bout, Galento felt unusually warm as Jimmy Frain administered a post-workout rubdown. It had been a torrid day, and Galento complained that the rubdown room was "terrifically hot." Against Frain's advice, Tony decided to cool off beside a water well, a shady spot where the fighters occasionally relaxed. Officials later reported that he may have consumed several quarts of milk after the workout, though it may have been apocryphal, hinting at the unhealthiness of milk for the beer-trained Galento. Although Jimmy Frain advised him to move away from the well, Galento stayed outdoors. Frain rubbed him with a towel.

"Gee," Galento said, "I'm drying up, but I'm cold."

Frain insisted that Galento move. Tony went inside and sat in an easy chair, his color poor. After dinner he decided to head to Orange to see his wife and son. They drove at sixty miles an hour, air cooling him further. He continued to complain of chills when he reached his tavern, and not even several games of darts, or a half dozen Tarzan yells, warmed him. Mary called Dr. Joseph Higi, who examined Tony and immediately sent him to the Orange Memorial Hospital.

Arriving shortly after 7:00 PM, Galento was placed in an oxygen tent. His temperature stood at 104.4 degrees and his pulse had risen to 120. Dr. Higi called Dr. Dean Marquis of the New York Post Graduate Hospital staff for a consultation.

Galento began to hack, his lungs and chest heaving to get air. Joe Jacobs, who had been summoned by Mary when Dr. Higi suggested Tony go to the hospital, stood by. He made a series of phone calls to Muggsy Taylor — the promoter for the Lewis–Galento fight — and Jules Aronson, head of the Pennsylvania Boxing Commission. Harry Mendel, Tony's sometime promoter and friend, announced to the press that Galento had bronchial pneumonia.

"Tony Galento right now is a very sick man and my sympathy first goes to the man," Mendel said. "While I feel for Herman Taylor, who through his efforts, has put over the finest promotion in his long and successful career, Mr. Taylor agrees with me that at a time like this, we do not measure monetary consideration or disappointment when a life is at stake. My sincere wish is for the unfortunate man and his speedy recovery."

Taylor, who stood to lose a $200,000 gate, traveled to Galento's bedside. Seeing Two Ton's weakened state, he broke down and wept outside his friend's room. The doctors ordered two blood transfusions. To shield Tony from the seriousness of his condition, two Orange policemen, Detective Sergeant Joseph McGinley and Patrolman Fred Milliman, donated blood in the next room. When nurses injected Tony with the transfusion, they told him the bottles contained liquid food. Repeatedly Tony was told he had a touch of the grippe.

But by the next morning the medical team held out little hope for his survival. His temperature climbed to 105.6 degrees. John Henry Lewis visited him and reached under the oxygen tent to shake hands. He told Tony to get well and Tony replied, "I will, I will." Afterward Lewis sent a candle to St. Venatius Catholic Church, where parishioners said masses for Galento's improvement. His mother, standing outside the doorway when her son received a third transfusion, fainted and had to be resuscitated. Muggsy Taylor officially canceled the Philadelphia fight and told the press he only wanted Tony to get better. Telegrams from around the country spilled into the hospital. Tommy Farr, a fellow contender, phoned. Max Baer called from California.

Joe Jacobs, speaking to reporters in a subdued whisper, confided that Galento faced the crisis that fevers inevitably brought with them. "His life is at stake and will be for the next thirty-six hours," he said. "Dr. Higi says we'll know then — one way or the other."

Visibly moved, according to the *Chicago Daily Tribute*, Jacobs added, "Please don't ask me any questions. I don't want to talk to anyone. Tony is very bad. That's all I can say."

The next morning Galento's temperature lowered. He also took a small serving of Mary's chicken broth. He asked after his son and demanded to know when he would be released. Mary told him, "Not for a few days." A few days turned into three weeks before Galento could get on his feet. By then his weight had dropped and he appeared shrunken and pale. During one treatment he asked Dr. Higi what the nurses were shooting in his arm.

"Why, it's only salt," Dr. Higi said.

"Is that the way to give a guy salt? Just tell Mary to put some more in my soup. I don't like that jabbing in my arm."

He began to take short walks in the hospital corridor. The papers issued a request from the Galento family that well-wishers stay away from the hospital. Fifteen people jammed his room one day before the nurses put a stop to it. They feared the excitement would cause a relapse. A month after he entered Orange Memorial, he left the hospital. He stayed home for a week before traveling to the Poconos, where his longtime friend Joey Dwyer, formerly of the Cincinnati Reds, had a mountain camp. From there he told reporters to "bring on Joe Louis." But he was weak and shaky, hardly the man, or boxer, he was before he won his "bout with dat bum ammonia."

JACOBS SLOWLY ladled Tony back into the ring after his illness. In a stroke of inspired maneuvering, they decided only to fight fighters who had lost to Louis. The idea, at least as Joe Jacobs outlined it, was to show that Tony could beat the fighters Louis had beaten. Critics, and some state boxing officials, also wondered if the plan did not revolve around putting Tony in with "tankers," men willing to see Galento's point of view without bothering with too many punches. In his first return bout after the illness — and after losing, according to one writer, eighty pounds before slowing building back up to 236 — Two Ton stopped Harry Thomas, a bruising elbow fighter from Michigan, in the third round. Twelve thousand fans watched the contest in Philadelphia's Convention Hall, and most reported that Thomas held the edge through two rounds. In the third, suspiciously one short of the four rounds Joe Louis required, Galento got his man. *The New York Times* reported that

> the crowd showed its disapproval in the third as Thomas went down five times, to the amazement of the onlookers, if not Galento. Newspapers were rolled up and hurled from all directions to the ring. Maybe Thomas was a target, too. Or both fighters. At any rate, as Thomas went up and down like a robot, the shower persisted and the roar of the aroused onlookers rolled across the arena.

The chairman of the Pennsylvania Boxing Commission, Jules Aronson, found the coincidence a bit too tidy and held the purses for an investigation. When he finally dispersed the monies, giving Tony seven thousand dollars, his richest payday yet, he warned Thomas to make his living elsewhere, barring him from fighting in Pennsylvania again. Nevertheless, Referee Tommie O'Keefe said that while Tony did not look as fast as he had in previous bouts, his punches still carried weight.

Next he fought Otis Thomas in St. Louis, a fight braided with controversy. Deliberately set in the "the West," out of the spotlight of New York, the bout went seven rounds before Tony was disqualified for low blows in the eighth. The managers, promoters, and boxing commissioners held an impromptu meeting at ringside, took a long look at the dollar signs, and recommenced the battle. Although observers gave the fight to Otis Thomas for the first seven rounds, suddenly he experienced a reversal. In the ninth round Tony landed a solid hook to Thomas's gut, and Thomas couldn't continue. Reporters wondered aloud if the fight had been rigged, but no one offered proof. Galento carried a whiff of cigar smoke and backroom dealing wherever he went. But he had also won seven bouts in a row, had challenged Louis nationally with a trip to Washington, where he posed with a ten-thousand-dollar bill as a wager and parroted, "I'll moida da bum," whenever the champ's name entered a conversation. Shortly after the Otis Thomas fight Two Ton knocked out Dick Daniels in an exhibition bout in Michigan with two hard rights to the heart and became a publicity landslide. He returned to Orange for a January match with Jorge Brescia, an Argentine who was called, ironically, the Mild Bull of the Pampas, a play on the name of his more famous countryman, Luis Angel Firpo, who had staged the remarkable bout with Jack Dempsey. After his first airplane ride, Galento stepped off the flight as temporarily famous as any man in the country. Reporters followed him wherever he went. He was copy. He was unavoidable.

JORGE BRESCIA, at 216 pounds, had passed his prime even though he was only twenty-four years old. He had boxed three good rounds against Joe Louis in the New York Hippodrome fight in 1936, even tagging the young future champ with a left hand that staggered the Brown Bomber, but three years in the life of a fighter is an eternity. A clever boxer,

Brescia was an acceptable choice for a test of Galento's skill and stamina. In sparring sessions Brescia handled George Nicholoson, a long-time Joe Louis sparring mate, with relative ease. Billy De Foe, Brescia's veteran trainer, claimed Brescia had never been in better shape. Abe Green, the New Jersey Boxing Commissioner, huddled with Louis Soresi, Brescia's manager, and Harry Mendel, the Newark promoter, and agreed to let the match take place in the Newark Armory. Called the "big drill shed" by locals, the Newark Armory held over nine thousand patrons on a good night and there was no reason to believe Galento wouldn't pack the place. Joe Jacobs, blustering and muttering, invited his friend and sometimes antagonist, Mike Jacobs, to witness the brawl. The Jacobs Boys, as the press called them, had a dozen different angles to play. Although Joe Jacobs and Galento wanted the Brown Bomber and a shot at the title, Mike Jacobs had dangled Max Baer, another of his fighters, as a possible match for Tony. Baer, a former champ and a colorful character in his own right, held significant drawing power, and would establish, once and for all, Galento's credentials as a serious contender. Mike Jacobs also had plans for matching the thirty-year-old Baer with a twenty-four-year-old, yoga practicing Californian named Lou Nova. Nova, with the looks of a matinee idol, appeared to be the finest, most promising young heavyweight around.

As it happened, Mike Jacobs might have saved himself the trouble of traveling the six or seven miles to Newark. Joe Louis, who booked himself a seat in the front row in order to take a look at the two contenders, might have also spent his night in a more entertaining venue. The only drama the evening held occurred before the fight, when neither man wanted to be the first to enter the ring. It required Chief Boxing Inspector P. James Pellerechia's intervention to unlock the stalemate, and through trickery and flattery he managed to get both men to climb under the ropes simultaneously. That snow job took longer than the fight. Charging off his corner stool and bellowing as he shot across the ring at the opening bell, Two Ton hit Brescia in the gut with a square left. Brescia answered with a weak right hand to Tony's temple, but the Night Stick socked the Argentine in the belly again, then again. The punches registered, taking the wind from Brescia, and Referee Whitey Healy ordered him to a neutral corner to compose himself. When the action recommenced, Brescia threw a left hook so hard he missed and followed his fist to the canvas. It appeared, some said, as if he had suddenly been handed an anvil.

Encouraged that he could penetrate Brescia's defense at will, Tony zeroed in on his opponent's stomach and struck him with a bull's-eye punch, a hook that went so deep into the lighter man's stomach that he would later be treated at a hospital. Before Brescia could straighten, Tony bull-rushed him, jamming another punch into his stomach. The Argentine crumpled like a plastic cup at the edge of a campfire, said one writer, in the end taking the count on all fours. Referee Healy stopped the fight one minute and forty-one seconds into the first round. As Healy counted, Galento wandered around a neutral corner waving and blowing kisses to friends and backers, mugging as only he could. Galento had won his ninth successive bout, and he had taken out Brescia in one round while Louis had required three. Over nine thousand customers had paid $16,850 to see Galento fight a capable, if somewhat recycled, opponent. To give his fans added value for their support, Two Ton remained in the ring for five or ten minutes after Brescia left, chatting and hamming it up, giving Tarzan calls and doing a fey curtsey to the cardinal points of the compass. Willie Ratner in the Newark paper said Galento, "Bowed hither and thither like a Presidential candidate." As he left the ring his foot went through a stair and the crowd loved him all the more for it.

Referee Whitey Healey went on record that Tony's punches would have decimated Louis if they landed with the same impact as they did against Brescia. Louis, for his part, did not find Two Ton Tony particularly fearsome. He told the press he could beat Galento with little difficulty. Mike Jacobs, though not impressed one way or another by the demonstration of Galento's powers, did take notice of the crowd's fascination with Tony. Galento was box office. Although understandably worried that a puncher of Galento's power could end the reign of his more skilled boxer, he also saw the pairing as inevitable. If the unthinkable occurred, and Galento managed to tag Louis with a left hook, the contract, any contract with the champ, gave Louis an immediate right to a rematch. Against Schmeling, Louis had already proven he could beat a man who had beaten him. Even if Galento somehow defeated Louis once, which was unlikely, the younger man would have an advantage in the second contest. No one, Jacobs thought, could beat Louis twice in a row at this point in the young fighter's career.

* * *

SEVERAL THOUSAND people swarmed Newark's Pennsylvania Station in late January when news spread that Two Ton Tony Galento was about to board the train for Detroit. Joe Jacobs had signed his boxer to fight Natie Brown in Detroit's Olympic Arena on February 3. Brown, a pug Galento had knocked out in 1932 after one minute and forty two-seconds of the first round at the Laurel Garden, posed nothing more than a workout for Tony, but Jacobs wanted his fighter busy. Besides, some critics still believed Galento had not fully recovered from pneumonia, and Brown might serve as further proof that the Night Stick was back. By keeping him active, and in the press, pressure built on Mike Jacobs to accept Galento for a heavyweight shot. Leslie E. Kinsey, a typical citizen of Kearny, New Jersey, wrote a letter to the editor of the *Star-Ledger* that put the matter squarely before the fight world.

> If Galento is the No. 1 challenger why isn't he given a chance? Why don't the writers give him proper credit? What is more needed in the fight game just now than a real, honest-to-goodness fight, instead of a running match? Louis would hit Tony many times undoubtedly, but Tony would require only one real smack to slow the Brown Bomber down to his own pace, and then the suckers who pay their good money would see another Dempsey–Wild Bull of the Pampas affair that would reinstate the fight racket materially. Is it too much to hope for?

Unfortunately the bout with Brown did more to undermine Galento's reputation than enhance it. Looking "a bit frayed," as one reporter described the 207-pound Brown, Galento's opponent managed only one punch of any significant voltage before hitting the floor ten times in four rounds. Galento, one writer said, "resembled a bull frog in a pan of milk." Joe Louis, who had shaken hands with Galento in the dressing room, told reporters, "He didn't look so good to me. I think I can take him." The Michigan Boxing Commission did not enjoy the fight nearly as much as the 8,547 fans who paid $16,318 to sponsor it. Frank MacDonell, a fiery ex-sportswriter who had been appointed boxing commissioner in January 1937 by then mayor, and later attorney general, Frank Murphy, suspended Brown and barred Tony Galento from boxing in Michigan again.

The decision backfired on MacDonell almost immediately. Cited for ruling with a high hand in several earlier incidents, the most prominent involving an allegedly fake fight between heavyweights Jimmy Adamick and Jack Trammell, the Galento–Brown ruling painted the forty-year-old MacDonell as a man of harsh judgments. In a fit of pique over the public reaction, MacDonell sent his resignation to Governor Frank Fitzgerald, and was nonplussed when the governor gladly accepted it and told the press "it was for the good of boxing in Michigan." The public rewarded the ex-commissioner with a horse laugh when he tried to retract his resignation, and as Galento and Brown left town, their purses finally collected, only MacDonell was without a paycheck.

* * *

BY CHANCE, or by intent, Joe Louis's manager, Mike Jacobs, happened to be vacationing in Florida at the time of the Washington's Birthday Abe Feldman fight. In addition to the concern Mike Jacobs might have harbored about pitting his boxer against a street thug like Galento, business matters also complicated the potential arrangement. When Mike Jacobs paired Joe Louis with another fighter under the management of his Twentieth Century Sporting Club — a boxing collective he managed — he took from both ends of the profit. Whether Jacobs wanted to match Louis with Galento remained beside the point. Galento fought under the promotional direction of Herman Muggsy Taylor of Philadelphia, and to let Galento in was to let Taylor in as well. To make the fight, the money had to be right. Taylor, moreover, had to agree to permit Mike Jacobs to promote the match. It took six hours of wrangling, and several blowups, before the Jacobs boys — Joe and Mike — emerged to tell reporters a deal had been struck. On February 27, 1939, they announced the Heavyweight Champion of the World, Joe Louis, had agreed to put his title at risk against Two Ton Tony Galento. They set the match tentatively for June, likely in New York. Galento, keeping to standard pricing for challengers to the belt, agreed to accept 17 percent of the gate receipts. Herman Taylor settled on 5 percent of the overall take. The entire party posed shaking hands and smiling for the papers.

For Tony Galento, setting the date for his showdown with Joe Louis began what was likely the sweetest period in his life.

He had money, fame, even a glimmer of a life — in the movies — beyond fighting. His son, One Ton, appeared in photographs with enormous boxing gloves on his hands. The World's Fair buzzed in his neighborhood and a million fans knew his name. It was his shot, and he knew it. He was twenty-nine years old, the "age of champions" some writers declared. Marvin Hart, Jack Sharkey, and James J. Braddock had all been twenty-nine when they won the championship. Three men had been older: Jack Johnson, 30; Jess Willard, 31; Ruby Bob Fitzsimmons, 34. His chance would not come again, but that it had come once, in the end, amazed even him.

JOE JACOBS leaked to the press that Tony Galento had devised a special method of pushing off the referee, then sinking his fist like a harpoon into the champion's hide. He failed to explain how it could be carried off, but it was an impressive image. He also let it be known that Tony planned to fight from an extreme crouch, making it difficult for Louis to time his punches. The technique, borrowed from Tommy Farr, who had given Louis such trouble in fifteen rounds, received endorsement from Teddy Broadribb, Farr's manager, who had arrived for the fight on the *Mauritanian*. Broadribb picked Louis to win, but said the contest could be close. His shipmate, a jovial bookmaker from Belfast named Hughie McAlevey, revered Dempsey above all other fighters, but disagreed with his hero by picking Galento to win if the fight went more than two rounds. McAlevey's only worry for the fight was that fresh air and exercise had taken away Tony's grit. "Tony could lick any of the heavies over the past fifteen years," he said. "Except, of course, Dempsey. Galento's by far the best man Louis has met. I'd stake my life that he's a better fighter than Schmeling was, yet Schmeling knocked out Louis."

The biggest rumor to fuel fight interest, however, revolved around the prospect of Two Ton making an initial charge and tackling Louis. Various columnists prophesied that Galento would punch Louis in the groin, disabling the champ and making him appear a coward if he did not continue. Others went on record that Galento promised a "Pier 6" brawl, a fight without rules, an elbow-whacking, head-butting affair that would become gruesome to watch. Joe Louis, speaking from Pompton Lakes, New Jersey, his favorite training camp, promised he would dance as rough as Tony wanted to dance. When Joe Jacobs heard Louis's statement, he quickly reminded the fight writers that Louis had a record, too.

"Sure, Galento is rough," the manager said, "but he's never been disqualified. Who did the low punching in the first Schmeling fight? I'll tell you if you don't remember. The fellow's name was Louis. Look up the official's slips at the Commission and you'll learn that Louis was warned and penalized several times for the blows. Why, just before the knockout Referee Arthur Donovan warned Joe for fouling. I think Louis knows he's licked if he doesn't get help. He's trying to intimidate the officials that Galento will violate the rules. I can't speak for Louis."

Asked directly by Joe William of the *Watertown Daily Times* about a quote saying he intended to fight dirty, Galento shook it off. "That gave the boys something to write about," he said, "but I'd be silly to deliberately go out and fight foul. I might get a bit rough at times, but after all, all people are paying big dough to see a fight, not two spooners in Central Park."

On the final day of training, Two Ton returned to Grouch's gym in Newark, his averred lucky spot. Grouch's gym, as boxing people knew, was actually a poolroom. He sparred eleven rounds, skipped rope, shadowboxed, and topped off the day with a ride around the area with his trainers, Jimmy Frain and Johnny Burke. He also received a telegram from Mrs. Ida B. Wise, president of the Women's Christian Temperance Union, who scolded him for his habits and publicly declared,

> Undoubtedly, many young Americans will be influenced by which man wins Wednesday night's fight. Millions of people in this country, not only church and temperance groups, but school people and others interested in youth welfare, have fought for decades and are still fighting against the habits of life which Galento lives. The W.C.T.U., however, is interested in the "living creed" of the men — it favors the clean-living Louis creed as opposed to the self-indulgence-in-things-harmful-to-you creed of Galento and his beer kegs.

Later that evening Tony stopped into the tavern to check on ticket receipts for the fight. Mary reported the count had exceeded $12,000. Nick Franco, president of the Tony Galento Association, reported a steady demand for extra tickets. They couldn't keep them in stock. Big money had arrived at last.

5

AT TONY'S TAVERN on Day Street in Orange, seven hundred people, jammed into every crevice, screamed at the conclusion of round one. Everything beautiful seemed possible. Tony might win. Orange, New Jersey, might be home of the Heavyweight Champion of the World.

For years Tony had begged for a chance to face Joe Louis and had kept a poster of the Brown Bomber over the bar. To amuse the press and friendly patrons, he often walloped the poster and shouted that he could "moida dat bum Louis!" During training he had invited the press to a tea party where his handlers screened film clips of Louis suffering knockdowns and batterings. The Galento team, however, cut their insults with comedy. Joe Jacobs called a press conference and made a formal request to disallow any sportswriters from helping the Brown Bomber back into the ring when and if Tony knocked him out of it. Jacobs did not want, he said, a repeat of the Firpo–Dempsey fight, where Dempsey received a hand back into the ring from the working press. Jacobs asked the New York Commissioners to instruct the first two rows of sportswriters to let Louis remain where he landed in the event he sailed out of the ring. If Louis happened to be rolling past, Jacobs continued, the writers should make no attempt to slow him down.

But that was for public consumption, to push the gate higher.

Alone and late at night, Tony often dialed Joe Louis's number in Pompton Lakes, New Jersey, where the champ trained. In those whispered conversations Galento told Louis what he intended to do to him in the ring. He called Louis every name in the book, questioned his manhood, talked about his race, made sexual references about Marva, Louis's wife. Years later, Galento apologized publicly for the phone calls and the two became friends, with Louis often visiting Tony's tavern. Louis eventually said of his bitter enemy, "There's no harm in him. He's just full of wind, like the barber's cat." But at the time the phone calls and mocking served as bluster to cover Galento's own insecurity. Galento and Jacobs believed they would thrive in chaos, unsettle the champ, and so they set about prying open Louis's deadpan expression. Unfortunately for Galento, it angered Louis, alerted him to his opponent in a way that proved a tactical error. Louis resolved to carry Galento, to cut him to ribbons, to make him pay for the insults the bartender threw at his feet. Never before or after did Louis betray such animus toward an opponent. But Galento had dogged him, and Louis intended to make him pay.

Now, at a little after 10:30 PM, Two Ton had hit Louis with his great left claw and all the previous tactics had been abandoned. Tony Galento, and every other son of Italy, had reason to believe he could hit him again. Tony possessed the natural leverage that makes a person a puncher. As awkward as he sometimes appeared in the ring, when his punches landed properly his entire body formed a hypotenuse between the floor and the opponent's chin. His position resembled a chair being propped against a door to keep out an intruder. He had knocked out plenty of men with a single punch. He had the knack.

IN HARLEM during the minute-long break between rounds fans looked carefully at one another over their radios and felt their stomachs tighten. Not King Joe, they told one another. Many did not share the press's dismissal of Tony Galento. They knew tough Italian kids. They did not doubt Galento for an instant, though Joe Louis, they understood, was in all ways the superior boxer. But when Louis entered the ring he carried them all with him, and they mistrusted the hope they placed in him. It was dangerous to hope too much; disappointment never failed to visit.

But they loved Joe and would never go back on him. After an earlier fight with Primo Carnera, John Roxborough and Julian Black, the Brown Bomber's managers, arranged an appearance by Joe Louis at the Savoy Ballroom at 140th Street and Lennox Avenue. In the light of a neon billboard, twenty thousand fans showed up to cheer Louis, clamoring for tickets inside. Dancers tried out the Shim-Sham Shimmy and the Lindy Hop as they waited. Louis's managers sent a squadron of cars to the front door, while Joe, in a darkened car, snuck in the back way. When the time finally came for Joe to appear in front of the mob, the building manager called it off. He worried that Joe's presence so close to so many admirers would be uncontrollable. They paid him his two-thousand-dollar appearance fee and let him slide out the side door.

In Harlem after the Schmeling victory black people climbed to the rooftops and threw tin cups, cans, and bottles to smash in the street. In Cleveland police employed tear gas to slow the people down. But it didn't work. Tenements sprouted tongues of white cloth, speaking messages written in paint down their sides. Joe Louis, Champ. Hitler Loses. Nazis Lose.

Now Joe Louis had been hit by Galento, a boxing scorpion with one great weapon but little else, and they wondered and kept their eyes busy. They had to stand with Louis, they understood. They sent thoughts out to him, encouraged him with short, quiet little exhalations. A few spoke sharply to children if they ventured too near the radio or threatened the transmission by the obstinacy of their bodies. Others called loudly, entreating Joe to get busy. They felt his anguish in their chests and in the slight shakiness that threatened their legs and put a minute tremble in their hands.

* * *

HEAVYWEIGHT championship fights are different from other spectator sports. More briefly, and more poignantly, a boxing match remains exquisitely balanced between hope and desperation. For the fan at the stadium the minute between rounds is simultaneously too short and far too long. In photographs snapped between rounds, nearly every spectator's arms extend as if to grasp bicycle handlebars, the excitement of combat transferred into them. They cannot abide contact with their neighbors; in the same instant, they crave confirmation that they have seen what they have just seen. So the fans turn and move and sway, their arms braced, and touching, and it all passes too quickly, too imperfectly; the senses cannot absorb it all. Then when they have finally accommodated themselves to inaction, the bell rings again, jerking the fighters to their feet, and they see the stool removed, the spray of the sponge flick an arc of liquid one last time on the boxer while the bucket rocks and a lip of water gums over the edge, the common, everyday splash incomprehensible under such circumstances.

AT THE BELL, the crowd in Tony's tavern quieted. You cannot listen to a broadcast and shout at the same time. Across the country, people bent forward, silent, listening to the trained voice of the announcer. When someone near the radio interrupted, or spoke, the listeners instinctively raised a hand, silencing the speaker. Forty million people leaned forward, their eyes focused somewhere distant, their imaginations pushing them into Yankee Stadium. Some had never seen a photograph of Galento; he existed as an Italian, a chubby bartender, and they imbued him with whatever characteristics they required to complete him. Likely, they had a surer image of Joe Louis, but what height he had, what bulk, how his gloves covered his hands, they applied in their imaginings. Silence trickled over the continent, moving westward as the transmission flowed to the Pacific. Across the nation cars became louder, dogs barked with more force, as the pools of silence linked and spread and the background noises amplified by comparison. Using car batteries to power their radios, or stealing the transmission from the local dry goods store, blacks in Mississippi and Missouri and Oklahoma listened to their great Joe Louis step forward for round two, and in spaghetti houses in Asbury Park, in Point Pleasant, in Cherry Hill, they stopped stirring pots to hear how Galento fared, to hear if he could pull off the unimaginable. When they resumed, they kept their spoons from the side of the vats, their twirling continuing in slowly, lazy tornadoes.

AS HE WALKED toward the center of the ring for round two, Tony Galento had already claimed a victory of sorts. The crowd understood it. He had gone toe to toe with Joe Louis, the pink of all heavyweights, and he had won a round, had actually tagged the great champion and sent him into the ropes halfway across the ring. For a five-foot-eight flabby Italian American, a mediocre boxer who had no hope but to fight with honor, he had done something courageous and fine. The fans in Orange felt Tony's triumph in their throats, blinked back tears to hear the description of their favorite son walking implacably across the ring, his mouth open, his chest pumping, his left hand containing the dreams of more people than he knew.

His sweat by now had turned his trunks the color of eggplant. His right eye had filled with swelling, but not seriously yet. His left hand had lost most feeling. His right probed ahead like a man separating the undergrowth so his favored hand could grab the missing item. His mouth open, he sifted the air around him, a baleen whale, his lips parted to let oxygen seep into his system. His legs, 27-inch thighs, 18½-inch calves, stumped forward. His forehead led the procession. Occasionally he punched his gloves together as he walked, a pug's habit, a sparring leftover, a demonstration of his willingness to begin again.

WHETHER HIS corner men had chided him, or whether he had simply sharpened his appetite, no one could tell, but Joe Louis came out for round two with deadly earnestness. At twenty-five years old, at the start of his prime, he demonstrated, with the casual grace of the young, why he dominated his generation of heavyweights. Circling slowly, his fists cocked and always ready, he punched Galento at will, his combinations flowing beautifully behind his powerful jab. His timing improved. His punches gained a rhythm, not like a dancer's rhythm, but like the hammer blows of a man roofing a house. He hit Tony with a right on the cheek and the twist and compression of the punch caused tiny blood vessels to rupture. Blood broke out red and bright and Louis, no fool, punched for the target. A red stripe grew and became permanent under Galento's nose, blood following the channel of his upper lip. Galento's right brow burst open eventually, too, and blood dripped over that cliff and clung to the opthalmic ridge, emptying finally into his sweaty eye.

But Louis hardly needed blood to ensure his victory. He had Galento now. He understood him. He began to measure him, sticking his left out and gauging the distance down his arm. For his part, Galento appeared hopelessly overmatched. He could not box. He had never been a boxer, and now, with the championship on the line, his lack of disciplined training, his inattention to technique, he could not match the great Brown Bomber. He accepted the pain, still moving forward. He tried to land his left, but he could not get close enough. Louis kept him off balance, peppering him.

Their bodies demonstrated the change in command. By the midpoint in round two, Galento slumped, became more sullen, while Louis crisply delivered punches. Here, at last, the magnificent Brown Bomber stepped forward and punched with a smooth efficiency that appeared effortlessly overwhelming. Through twelve years, and twenty-four defenses, he would administer succinct beatings such as this one, and no one who knew his style, his grace, exhibited surprise when the fight began to follow its destined choreography. A few people throughout the stadium backed slowly into their seats, as if settling in for a second act. Now the fight made sense. Now events followed the proper script, and they watched with a mixture of pity for Galento, who foolishly elected to endure such punishment, and with admiration for Louis, his deadliness as stylish as a musician finally breaking free with his chosen instrument. He had done this before, they saw. Oh, that's it, people said, recognizing Louis's superb competency. Many began to wince as Galento's face caught Louis's hands and sent them back with blood.

IN ORANGE, people listening to the fight found something to engage their hands. They pulled at a thread or stooped to snatch a piece of paper from the floor. This is what they feared. Suddenly the ring announcer seemed too loud, too strident, and they yearned to ask if he really called it correctly, or if some mistake could not be possible. A few, unquestionably, felt the gloomy satisfaction of things not turning out as they hoped. They did not feel sadness, or pity, but a gratified orderliness in their lowest expectations coming to fruition. How could someone they knew, someone who tended bar and raised chickens and smoked cigars while riding on a sidecar motorcycle, who threw out the first pitch for the Newark Bears' game, or blew the starter's pistol for a six-day bicycle race — how could he become champion? If Tony Galento could be champion, then they might also be more than they thought, and that was the hardest thing to believe. They listened, but their stomachs had accepted the defeat long ago, and they dared not look around them for fear others would see into their anticipation of loss, and they would be found out, and they would be traitors to the hope that surrounded them.

* * *

SECONDS FROM the end of round two, Joe Louis knocked Tony Galento off his feet. Louis landed a straight right hand to Galento's face and when Tony flinched and crumpled from the impact, Louis caught him with a crisp left hook on the point of the chin. The New Jersey Night Stick, who had never been down in a prizefight, who had kept this morsel of pride alive through one hundred fights, perhaps a thousand rounds, took the shock of the punch straight backward and went down on his backside. The punch sent white spray from Galento's head into the ringside light. Men in direct line behind Galento instinctively held out their hands to brace him, despite his distance and height above them. His head snapped back like a mechanical boxer, a toy whose chin attaches to a spring and emits a wheezing sound. The crowd screamed. Louis stepped back. Galento jumped to his feet, his face drawn, his shock evident. Referee Donovan stepped between the men, held Galento's gloves for an instant, then let the fight resume.

GALENTO'S FACE betrayed his fear and astonishment. He had once flown out of the ring trying to hit a man, but he had never, even in training, been knocked down. Critics believed his weight and bottom-heaviness made him impossible to put on the canvas. Throughout his career he endured the unspoken prejudice of a crowd watching a fat man's pain. His flesh made him impervious;

he did not bruise and ache the way thinner men did. Joseph Donovan, a beat writer for the Newark papers, said "the New Jersey Ogre's build is prehistoric man rather than a modern obese person. He resembles the statue of Neanderthal Man by the world famous sculptor, Frederick Blaschke, in Chicago's Field Museum. One would get a fine comparison. Both are powerful wreckers of flesh and bone when aroused. Both have short, thick muscular necks, which is proof they can absorb punishment. Their necks, arms, and legs are the same, solid, powerful — and hairy, too."

It is possible that Galento believed such nonsense himself, but now Joe Louis had taken that away, deprived him of the illusion of invincibility. With one punch Tony Galento had become another pug who had hung on too long. He could never say about himself that he had remained on his feet if nothing else. That had been lifted from him by a nigger, a moolignon, a black sonofabitch.

GALENTO SWUNG wildly, trying to make up in violence what he had lost in precision. For a moment he became the enraged little brother wind-milling his arms at his antagonistic older sibling. Then the fight settled again, and Louis began the busy occupation of hitting the fat man. A left jab. A right cross. A left, a left, another left. Before Galento could react, the left jab smacked him in the nose, on the cheek, on the suction cup of his eye. The ending had become inevitable. Galento's head woodpeckered back and forth with the sting of each blow.

For an instant, if one squinted, it appeared Louis's hands could not rid themselves of Galento's face. Two Ton's body had become flypaper; Louis, by some extraordinary means, might be pulling his punches away from Galento and jerking the fat man forward. But that was illusion, one created by the speed of Louis's hands, the accuracy of his punches. Fans at ringside felt suddenly sorry for the challenger. This was the consequence for reaching above himself. Louis hit Galento as he liked, and Tony trundled forward, his hands down, his face accepting the fists. What had been spirited and fun only minutes before now had the dismal appearance of an animal blundering forward despite the anticipation of pain. Louis had no options; he hit Galento in combinations and drew him forward into his arc. Galento followed.

AT THE BELL, the men returned to their corners and the crowd, aware of Louis's dominance, tasted the proper measure of salt in their mouths. Dunphy, the ringside radio announcer, wondered aloud how much more Galento could take. It may have been a premature statement, but it was nevertheless true that Tony had been hit hard and often. Other than the great left hook in the first round, he had landed next to nothing. Louis remained clearly in control. The knockdown, it seemed to those who watched, broke Galento somehow. He could no longer swagger or boast. If boxers must accept their mortality more sharply than others, then Tony Galento's moment of understanding had arrived.

Whitey Bimstein, who knew cuts and knew what to do about them, jammed a pad against Galento's brow as soon as his boxer arrived at his corner. Bimstein pressed hard, trying both to staunch the bleeding and to hide the blood from Art Donovan, the referee. Bimstein recognized an ugly, fight-ending cut when he saw one. He also suspected that Tony would fight blind the rest of the bout, his right eye flickering with a rain of blood visiting it, his right side open to concealed attack by the Bomber. Louis's left jab, especially, could not be given a better, sweeter, target.

JOE JACOBS shouted at Tony, pulling his fighter's trunks out and trying to bellow air into his soft lungs. Galento had always been a cocky sonofabitch, and Jacobs appealed to his pride, his enmity for Louis, his quick pain at being ignored by the boxing cognoscenti. Simultaneously, Jacobs assured Galento it was okay. Everything was okay. They had arrived at round three, and his boy was in it, Tony was in it, keep swinging, press him, dodge, you fucking sonofabitch, swing that left, club him, okay, okay, breathe. Next to Jacobs, Jimmy Frain said little and ministered to his boyhood friend. Among all the men and women who had come and gone, the managers, the fakers, Jimmy Frain had stood by his buddy. Now he had seen his indomitable friend knocked on his hind end for the first time in his life. Through a hundred fights Jimmy Frain had never seen that occur, and now, standing over his friend, he felt a quiet sadness, a worry that Tony Galento had at last met his match.

6

AT RINGSIDE the front rows anticipated Galento's ending. Now everyone became an expert. The ending that had become obvious transformed itself in people's minds to an ending they had predicted. Too much, they said of Louis. After the second Schmeling fight, John Kieran of the *New York Times* put Louis's prowess in doggerel:

> As hinted by many including this bard,
> The Shuffler, J. Louis, hits too bloomin' hard.
> And all I can think of, and all I can mutter
> Is: Louis is simply too utterly utter!

Kieran had been matched by J. McTernan, an avid fight fan and amateur poet, who sent this offering to the *Newark Star-Ledger* on behalf of Galento.

The boys call him Two Ton Galento
And he is a pretty tough gento
If you don't think so and you really must know
Please read this little memento.
You know how he got that sock?
Why he takes a half barrel of bock,
Lifts it over his head and so it is said
He carries it twice round the block.
There are no miles of road work for Tony
He'd rather eat home made bologny.
And train always near his seidel of beer
And gobble his wife's macaroni.
But when he meets Louis I betcha
All of the dough you can getcha,
That he ties "That Bum" Joe in a pretty brown bow
And sends him back home on a stretcha.

Far from poems of any kind, Louis, on his stool before round three, breathed smoothly, Chappie Blackburn whispering in his ear. Blackburn, a former fighter himself in the days of backroom matches, a man with a drinking condition who had shot two men and his own wife in 1909, a man who trained Louis though every fight until he could no longer climb the four steps into the ring, spoke quietly, his tone the whisper of a man gentling a horse. While John Roxborough, a former numbers runner and Detroit sportsman (but also a philanthropist who sent Detroit black youths to college and underwrote the costs of athletic teams), and Julian Black, who kept a series of Louis scrapbooks that would become famous in boxing lore, looked after Louis's money and career, Blackburn tended Louis's heart. Now he massaged his fighter's pride, his confidence, bolstering him with the patter of boxing phrases.

You got him. You got him now. Just keep going, just keep jabbing, slide, slide that step out right, you keep moving, keep that hand up, guard when you drop your right, follow it, follow it, he's done now, he's done.

The words meant little. Blackburn and Louis called each other Chappie, shared confidences, understood one another as only men can who know what it is to stamp back fear and injury inside a ring. The tone of Blackburn's words took all the other voices, the crowd shouts, the calls for peanuts, beer, the smash of camera bulbs as they dropped, and funneled them into quiet confidence. Blackburn served as the ring father, the man who Louis respected more than all others. When his natural father had appeared after the Braddock fight, Louis had no need of him. He had Blackburn, and the tone of Blackburn's voice, even here in Yankee Stadium, provided steady encouragement and insulated him from every possible distraction. Only after Blackburn died several years later did fighting become work for Louis. Before that, with Blackburn's voice in his ear, his career had been something to carry to this older man, a fellow fighter who understood his younger charge as completely as any man could.

Listening to his trainer, the Brown Bomber's ribs and chest rose and fell beneath his calm face. He had put Galento down, and like a man reaching with his foot to kill a spider he had mortally injured a moment before, he had every intention of finishing the job as efficiently as possible.

Across the ring, Louis saw the backs of three men ministering to Galento. You can tell who is winning a fight by the level of activity in the corner between rounds. Louis had brought those busy hands to Galento, and he intended to finish things in the next several minutes.

REFEREE ART DONOVAN visited Galento's corner and bent to examine the cuts sustained in the first two rounds. Whitey Bimstein kept a gauze pad on Galento's brow, the most vicious of the several ruptures on his fighter's face, while Joe Jacobs talked his jabber to keep the referee distracted. Blood had seeped into Galento's right eyelid, filling it and making it thick. Galento also breathed heavily, wheezing in hungry gulps. A championship heavyweight bout would not be halted under such relatively benign circumstances, but Donovan did not imagine the fight could go on much longer. Galento's expression held the surprised dullness of a man who had tackled too much, but still had inescapable work ahead of him.

Twenty seconds before the third round commenced, Donovan asked Galento's corner how their man felt. Their answer did not clear the crowd noise, but their movements asserted his readiness. Bimstein pinched hard on the broken brow ridge and then glued the sagging skin together with a smear of petroleum jelly. The jelly mixed with blood and turned a dark crimson; liquid flowed beneath the skim of jelly like water slipping under ice. Galento climbed to his feet and stood ready to answer the bell. His breath came in rapid pants. Sweat rolled through his eyes and brought salt to his lips and to the gouges on his face. The memory of the knockdown seared him, but its painful truth, its indisputable reality, ached in him like heartbreak. He watched Louis's corner unfold like a flower, the cornermen peeling back to reveal Louis. The Brown Bomber stood and checked his traction, his shoes scraping a small, bullish swipe on the canvas. Galento leaned forward as well, his body tipped toward the center of the ring, where Art Donovan raised both arms, ready.

THE BELL for round three rang and both men advanced, their fists moving in their unconscious styles as if the fight could be fought through air. Louis came out for the third clearly feeling better. He moved crisply, circling and angling, while Galento, still frog-hopping, followed. Louis now had the fight figured out; he could see how it had to go, and he maneuvered Galento carefully, preparing him for the finish. He jabbed. He hit Galento in the gut, crossed him with a right to the head. The punches landed. Always a fearsomely accurate puncher, Louis had a large, vulnerable target in front of him and he suspected the second round had damaged his opponent severely. He moved confidently forward. His feet, always anchored, shuffled slowly, his stance a classic half turn to offer his opponent less to hit, just a slice of ribs and two fists relentlessly pouring outward.

From Galento's corner, Joe Jacobs shouted for Galento to crouch and offer less of a target. He could also, the thinking went, jack-in-the-box up and hack at Louis in one enormous lunge. The tactic had worked in the first round, but now it shackled Galento, made him even less mobile than usual.

Several fighters had been successful against Louis by fighting in a crouch, most notably Tommy Farr, a Welsh coal miner from Tonypandy, whose sisters held bundles of leeks as he fought, hoping the onions would bring him luck. Perhaps the leeks worked, because Farr strung the new champion along through fifteen rounds and nearly beat him by decision.

The squatting tactic, natural for Farr, did not fit Galento comfortably. After the fight Galento complained that his corner had given him bad advice by counseling him to fight tucked down, but he advanced with his head lowered despite his sense that it was a mistake to do so. Now, in the third, he bulled ahead, sometimes bringing his head up under the Bomber's chin. Louis answered by clicking punches off Galento's face, forcing the shorter man to keep his distance. Several times Louis gauged his punches perfectly, and caught Galento's head dangling at waist level, punching him fiercely, then stepping away. Galento's head twisted in response to the punches like a man staring down at the ground trying to find something he had lost. And like many men losing at a bet, or contest, Galento succumbed to the sweetly satisfying pleasure of accepting pain. By welcoming it, by watching one's funds run down through a blackjack table, or by offering no resistance when struck, the loser gains a perverse victory. It attempts to turn loss into something so exquisitely painful that it steals the pleasure from the winner. The danger, naturally, is that the pain becomes the object of the contest, and to be hit more purely, to bleed more deeply, is a sort of rapture. Galento bobbed and moved and took Louis's fists. His heart moved somewhere else, and Louis, keenly aware, hammered him more viciously.

NOW THE CROWD leaned forward, eager to witness the ending. This, after all, was the reason for coming. If the crowd could not watch an upset victory by Galento, an unlikely miracle, then it contented itself with hoping for a memorable ending. The question now rested in *how* the thing would be done, not if or when. Tony's fans, the men and women who marched him in brass bands to fights in Philadelphia and in Newark, watched out of loyalty. Other fans, those who pulled for Louis, or who had no special interest either way, waited to see the final stab. Such moments held a deadly fascination, like watching a man working next to a saw, his back turned, his proximity to the turning blade riveting and appalling at once. The fight no longer held the aspect of sport; the punches had become butchery. Forty thousand people in the stadium, forty million listeners on radio, wanly smiled to see or hear Tony receive his beating. Nothing personal in it. Tony's blood was not their own, and that was cause for celebration, cause to appreciate the safety of the flock or school, cause to feel gratified at one's own survival.

IN THE CENTER of the ring, midway though the round, Joe Louis began to throw a left. In dropping his hand slightly to gain leverage, his right hand also dropped a millimeter. A line drawn between the two men at that point would have been a perfect schematic; their shoulders, as Galento prepared his own left, had precisely the same slant. They might have served as dance partners; or, better still, as a shadowboxing dybbuk that had come alive to attack the reflection of each man. Two Ton Tony, ducking and reaching for leverage, let go the left hand that would bring him fame for the remainder of his life. It beat Louis to the punch, and collided with the Bomber's chin, snapping it to Louis's left and making the champ's head recoil from the impact. For an instant — an instant captured on film, but now lost, according to some old-timers — Louis left the ground. Galento's punch lifted the Brown Bomber from the canvas, the force sending him inches above the ring, his feet rocked back like check marks. Then Louis crumpled. Tony's follow-through carried him halfway around and Louis, spinning with the force, screwed into the ground and fell backward, his left hand groping out to brace himself, his left shoulder taking the brunt of the tumble. Galento, in what would become one of several famous still photographs from the fight, shucked his hands down to his sides, opened his mouth and stared at the fallen Louis, and felt what it would be like to be Heavyweight Champion of the World.

THIS MOMENT made Tony Galento, and crushed him in the same instant. Forever afterward he would be "the man who nearly pried the crown off Joe Louis's head." His feat, while formidable, became his curse. Perhaps it would have been better to lose utterly, to achieve nothing memorable, because now, with one punch, he entered history more solidly than if he had gone down and stayed down in round two. He became a footnote, a flash, a moment of promise he could never fulfill. At a testimonial at a Robert Treat restaurant in Orange three decades later, at every cocktail party, meeting of men, bar, sporting event, at each mention of boxing or courage, he heard his name massaged, and examined again, Galento the Great, the guy who boxed Joe Louis and put the Bomber down in round three. No one could have imagined how the moment would cling to him, consume him, eat at him. His punch proved a dinner pass for the remainder of his life, an infallible introduction that came to mean, in his hearing, a bum, a loser, a guy famous for missing his chance. In Joe Louis's long career it was a hiccup, nothing else. In Galento's life it became the punch line to an eternal joke, the glimmer of a championship held for two seconds.

LOUIS STAYED down only a moment. Referee Donovan's hand did not strike one on his count before the champ had jumped back on his pins. Across the nation, though, people exploded. Galento had done it. He had knocked down the champ. All his bragging and bluster, all the stupidity and infantilism of his campaign, had been redeemed by the purity of his accomplishment. Regardless of what occurred next, no one would forget him. Other men had knocked down Louis, but none since he had been the champ. And never had such an improbable challenger, a man with so little claim as a contender, carried off something so miraculous. In that instant before Joe Louis climbed to his feet, Tony Galento had provided the nation with a glimpse of the greatest upset victory in boxing history. For an instant he stood in front of the stadium spectators, his Orange cronies, his family, the millions of radio listeners, as the champ of the world.

THE CROWD in that instant stood open-mouthed, screaming, their faces frozen in the white aluminum light of flashbulbs, their eyes fresh with passion. Even the vendors turned to the ring, their spins as coordinated as so many compass needles swinging to true north. Peanut transactions stopped, suspended, while the police horses woke to the throb of crowd noise slipping out of the stadium. Their ears flicked and their meaty hooves clomped richly on the cobblestone. A miracle, really. Unlike spectators at theater performances, or concerts, the fans had not attended to watch an event. They came, instead, to witness two men living a portion of their lives, and in that way joined them inside the ring. The crowd hooted its delight, screamed Tony's name, believed perhaps they had arrived at this point in time to witness the greatest moment in a man's life. The great bum, the fat, beer-guzzling Orange boy, had redeemed them all, had given meaning to their associations, however slender, and as soon as Louis stood, they turned to one another, their eyes seeking to confirm the pleasure of the moment.

BUT THIS was Joe Louis. He passed by Referee Donovan's shoulder, moving forward and looking for Galento. Tony came at him again, but he could not follow up his knockdown punch. His punches lost any pattern. Two Ton Tony could not find the key again. It had disappeared as quickly as it had arrived, a flash knockdown, a collision of a single instant, a movement forward by Louis, the slashing left by Galento, the perfect reckoning of both. After decades in the ring, a hundred fights, a thousand sparring rounds, after ridicule and jeering, Tony Galento had reached a moment of perfection. Had he been a more introspective man, he might have consoled himself with the knowledge that he had achieved something rare and pure, but he was a man of appetite and excess.

GALENTO'S FAMILY members watched like bingo players waiting for a last number — tense and wild-eyed, happy in a way they would know only a few times in their lives. Tony had done it; he had knocked down Louis. If fate now would be generous, fair, kindly inclined, they would have a champion carrying their blood. The family lifted their arms, pressed their neighbors, waited with astonished and happy eyes. It could be, it could be, it could be.

IN GALENTO'S corner, the boys screamed themselves hoarse. Who can blame them for celebrating one brief moment, a transcendent instant that would not likely come to any of them again? Joe Jacobs would die in less than a year's time. Returning to New York City from Galento's tavern, where he and the Night Stick had posed for a newsreel, Jacobs felt tightness in his chest. Harry Mendel, promoter and Newark gadabout, rushed him to the office of Dr. Nardiello, where Jacobs underwent a thorough examination. Jacobs said he felt much better, but Dr. Nardiello sent him to Dr. La Rotonda, a colleague on Fifth Avenue, for a cardiogram. After taking off his shirt for the examination, Jacobs slumped over in a chair and died before doctors could save him. He was forty-three years old.

Joe Jacobs's death would rock Tony Galento both personally and professionally. He wept when he heard the news. To reporters he said, "I've lost the best pal I ever had. He was like a father to me and a very understanding manager. He gave me the helping hand I'd been looking for for years."

As they sat shiva, people from the fight game told stories. They told of the time Jacobs drove through Greenwich Village in a cab and tried to spit his cigar out the window, but his store-bought teeth followed and he had to stop the cab and search for his choppers in the gutter. Bill Henry from the *Los Angeles Times* remembered seeing Joe Jacobs drive a team of white horses through the Brandenburg Gate in Berlin, down the Unter den Linden, while his Aryan cabby slumbered peacefully beside him, Jacobs' vest pocket stuffed with cigars he had smuggled through customs. Dorothy Parker wrote a tribute to him called "Yussel the Muscle." And naturally they remembered his contributions to the English language: "We wuz robbed," and "We should've stood in bed."

And Whitey Bimstein, who presided over the careers of hundreds of boxers in Stillman's Gym into the 1950s, and who watched as television consumed the small boxing venues with its ubiquitous blue light, would move to the next job, the next gash of blood, but he would always remember the Louis–Galento fight, the stroke of Galento's left hand as it aced the Bomber in round three. His fate left him to appear as a footnote in matches of the 1930s and '40s and '50s, a good guy with a sponge, a man who knew how to close a rupture, a trainer who, as a boxer himself, always refused to train.

For Jimmy Frain the moment proved his lifetime. He had devoted his life to his friend, and this was payment. He was the sidekick, the second fiddle, the quiet one. When the government divided Orange by running the interstate through it, decimating the parishes and making it a glimpse of urban decay for the tens of thousands of commuters who passed by it each day from western New Jersey, Jimmy Frain disappeared. A few old people in the sausage palaces remembered him, or at least recalled a tall, thin man beside Two Ton Tony Galento. Oh, Jimmy, they said. Quiet. Never married. Not really much to say about him. Is he dead?

IN THE LAST seconds of round three, Louis connected with a right, a left to the body, another right. Galento waded through the punches, trying to ignore them, trying to find the punch that had lifted Louis, but the cumulative weight of the Bomber's blows began to sag him. Louis continued punching, moving adroitly until the round ended, his corner grabbing him as soon as he approached. They reprimanded him for his sloppiness and for his hastiness in getting back up so quickly. Once a fighter is down, he may as well stay down for a full nine count. Louis should have learned that in the Braddock fight when he had been floored by an uppercut in the first round. When Blackburn shouted to remind him to take a count when he was knocked down, Louis said famously, "What, and let him get all that rest?"

Chappie Blackburn studied the Bomber's eyes and found them clear and bright. He had his wits; that was apparent immediately. He began framing the younger man's face with his hands, moving and talking, wiping sweat and jelly off his man's brows, keeping the eyes free of mess. After the Schmeling fight, which was the only bad beating Louis would endure for years, Blackburn said, "Every fighter, to become a great fighter, must take at least one good licking. If he can do that and learn at the same time, he'll be pretty, pretty good."

That stage of Louis's career had ended, but Blackburn understood his charge's heart. He had vanquished Schmeling, nearly crippling the man in the process, and he would vanquish Galento. Blackburn did not like that Galento had tagged his boy with a left, but every fighter is hit. No one can stop that. The trick, he knew, had something to do with knowing you could win. The same punch, delivered under different circumstances, might have spelled the ending for his guy. But Blackburn saw that his man's eyes meant business, and that wherever the Bomber had gone in that fall to the ground, he had returned now.

AT RINGSIDE THE swells turned to one another, their eyebrows up, their expressions open and happy. The sonofabitch, they said. That Galento. Here, at last, something unexpected had happened. As much as people had gassed about the fight, no one, deep down, expected Galento to put Louis on the floor. Sure, it was theoretically possible, but come on. They had the happy feeling of buying something cheap at an auction and discovering later that the item had substantial value. Here they sat at ringside, first class, while tickets for other fights, ones that had better arguments behind them, had been harder, and more expensive, to come by. Some of the men thought of a friend, a buddy, a fight fan they knew, and wondered how burned that fellow would feel, how chagrined, that he had missed the most exciting fight in years. Then they shook their heads and concentrated on the ring in front of them. Goddamned Tony, they thought and shook their heads again.

In the bleachers, the cheap seats, the Italians, the Galento fans, felt a deep, quiet pride in their guts. Inexplicably, they felt both tender and vindicated, as though they could punch someone and hug him in separate pulses of feeling. Some felt a sense of piety or reverence, cautiousness that they should not hope too much, not move too much, for fear the sublime spell would pass. Things did not happen this easily. Life did not taste this sweet. They had a saying — don't spit into Heaven. One did not tempt fate, did not swagger before God. And some of them, perhaps, wondered why they had come, what they had honestly hoped for, because victory — solid, defining conquest — had never been part of their lives.

7

IN 1828 THOMAS "DADDY" RICE, a white southern minstrel, saw a crippled black stable hand named Jim Crow doing a song and dance called Jumping Jim Crow. Rice bought the man's clothes and began working the dance into his act. He did the dance in blackface, starting a craze that led to a wave of blackface minstrel singers both before and after the Civil War. Historians are uncertain how the Jim Crow act and dance became associated with racial segregation laws, but it likely served as a general term of derision, a poke at the gimpy, laughable fool who dances for others' entertainment. Rastus or Sambo, other black cultural symbols, might have worked as a term of mockery as well.

Another theory, not far removed from the suggested origin provided by the crippled stable hand, suggests abolitionist newspapers began using the term after the Civil War. What the newspapers meant by it, or how it became married to the rules stipulating the segregation of water fountains, public eateries, or other institutions, is not particularly clear.

UNDER ALABAMA'S Jim Crow rules, no white female nurse would be required to serve in a room housing black men. Black and white men could not play together in a billiard room. Textbooks in schools could not be traded between races. In Florida marriage between a white person and a Negro, or between a white person and a person of Negro descent to the fourth generation inclusive, was forever prohibited. Libraries in North Carolina created and maintained a separate place for the use of colored people, but no colored militia group could be established where white troops remained available. In South Carolina no white child could be surrendered by right of guardianship, natural or acquired, to a Negro. In Georgia, blacks and whites had separate graveyards; similarly, white blind people lived in isolation from black blind people, if both required assisted living. Jim Crow prevented vendors of wine and beer from selling to both black and white customers in the same room. Telephone booths, fishing lakes, and showers in mining offices all required adequate segregation. Louisiana, in the early part of the twentieth century, called it a crime for a white and black man to share a boxing ring.

IN A THREE-YEAR span, from 1916 to 1919, in what has been called the "Great Migration," over half a million blacks fled the South. Another million left in the 1920s. During the Great Depression, when black sharecroppers were turned off the land in vast numbers, thousands of them joined relatives and friends in Chicago, Detroit, Pittsburgh, New York, and Los Angeles. The Barrows — Joe Louis's family — were swept up with them. Among the poorest families near Buckalew, Alabama, the Barrows never owned the land they lived on, and endured grinding racism made legal by Jim Crow. They moved to Michigan and began working in the burgeoning automobile industry.

Many black migrants were pushed out of the South by a series of natural disasters, such as floods and the boll weevil scourge that devastated cotton crops from Texas to Georgia. Other blacks traveled to the North searching for jobs created by the labor shortage during World War I and the truncated emigration from Europe to the United States in the 1920s. They also fled persecution and murders, lynchings and criminal social practices. What they found in the North, though not a "promised land," at least promised freedom from the more overt forms of Jim Crow. Many white city dwellers bitterly resented the influx of blacks, and violent race riots erupted all over the nation from 1890 to 1945. Major ones occurred in East St. Louis, Houston, Chicago, and Tulsa in the years 1917 through 1921. In nearly every case black people defended themselves and their families against roving mobs of white racists.

BILLIE HOLIDAY, the most famous black nightclub singer of the era, joined Count Basie's band in

1937, then moved to Artie Shaw's white orchestra in 1938. Few black singers jumped the color line in that period. In 1939 she took an engagement at the Café Society (Downtown), an interracial nightclub in Greenwich Village. The club became fashionable among intellectuals and the haute monde, and the political left found meaning in her singing. On April 20, 1939, approximately two months before the Louis–Galento fight, she recorded *Strange Fruit* for Commodore Records. The song, which described "strange fruit" hanging in a sycamore tree, delivered a haunting ballad about lynching. Holiday did not intend the song to be hypothetical. Lynching continued throughout the South during the 1930s, with schoolchildren let out for the day to participate, and with the teeth and ears of the victims sent to state governors for souvenirs.

LOUIS'S MOTHER moved to Detroit where Joe, her seventh child, spent the money given to him for violin lessons on boxing instruction. A poor student, he wound up in a tech school, where he apprenticed in cabinet building. Eventually he became a coal and ice deliveryman, then wandered into the booming auto business. While working on the assembly line at Briggs Manufacturing, Louis arranged to spar with Olympic boxer John Miller, who knocked him down seven times. But Louis returned day after day, and eventually began winning matches.

After fifty-eight amateur bouts, he met a black Detroit entrepreneur named John Roxborough. Roxborough was a man of contrasts: he was a bail-bondsman, a numbers runner, and, to some degree, a politician. He underwrote college educations for many young blacks in Detroit, and gladly supported black teams and athletes. When he met Louis, Roxborough asked the young man his name.

"Joe Louis Barrow," Louis said.

"Too long," Roxborough said. "We'll go with Joe Louis."

PRESIDENT COOLIDGE kept an electric horse in the White House, a mechanical contraption that he could adjust to various gaits by changing speeds on a motor underneath the saddle. With the touch of a button he could change from a trot to a gallop, from a gallop to a canter, from a canter to a pitching motion. Called "Dobbin" by the press, and purchased at a price of $700, the horse answered the president's need for exercise. Otto Panzer, a physical instructor at Manhattan's Whitehall Club during that period, claimed "No liver, high or low, lazy or somnolent or set in its ways, can withstand the persuasions" of the electric horse.

Coolidge's example proved so compelling that other titans of Wall Street followed his lead. John D. Rockefeller, working out at the Whitehall Club, preferred an electric camel, a specially designed apparatus that required the rider to sit in a saddle, put his feet in the stirrups, then endure a lurching, circular trot that replicated, according to its designers, the nauseating gait of the "living ship of the desert." Followed by a good lunch and a rubdown, electric rides sent a man back to work with a new snap to his step and hat brim.

Joe Louis preferred real horses. For Louis, horseback riding conferred much more than exercise. In July 1938, a year before the Galento bout, he participated in the first United States Negro Horse Show at the Utica Horse Club outside of Detroit. He rode a horse named MacDonald's Choice and took third place, winning a yellow ribbon in the five-gaited saddle class. The victory paid fifteen hundred dollars. To participate as a black man in equestrian events in the late 1930s marked the champ as someone who had arrived. He sincerely loved horses, but riding also placed him indisputably in the upper class of American society, a lifetime away from his origins in the cotton fields of Alabama. He purchased a $2,500 saddle horse from Bing Crosby, in addition to two other mounts, Jocko and Flash, from local stables. Flash, a demon horse by Louis's own description, could only be ridden by Louis and the trainer he employed. After purchasing custom riding togs for his young wife, Marva, he sent her to the famous equestrian academy in French Lick, Indiana, where she remained for six weeks, learning to ride both straight and sidesaddle, on three-gaited and five-gaited horses.

ON JUNE 23, 1937, the day after Joe Louis knocked out James "Cinderella Man" Braddock to become Heavyweight Champion of the World, Alabama social workers notified Louis that his father, Munroe Louis Barrow, had been kept alive for more than two decades in the Searcy Hospital for the Negro Insane in Mount Vernon, Alabama. Joe Louis had believed his father dead; Lily, his mother, had told him that his father died twenty years before, not long after he had been committed in 1912. She had married a second man, a sharecropper like her first husband, who moved the family north to Detroit, joining the migration of black workers to the north in 1923, the year cotton prices sank to eleven cents a pound.

Joe claimed no knowledge or recollection of his father, and did not go to Alabama to meet him. Instead he dispatched his oldest sister, Susie, to investigate. She returned and verified that the inmate, whose pictures from that time show him to be a bland, somewhat dazed man in denim overalls, could be no one else. The strong family resemblance, and the peculiar circumstances of his incarceration, made his identity unmistakable. In fact, Susie reported, Joe's notoriety in winning the championship had been the breath that restored Munroe Louis Barrow to life. Chambers County's Sheriff Lane, while escorting a new patient to Searcy Hospital the day after the title fight, mentioned to a hospital official that he recalled bringing Joe Louis's dad, Mun, to the same hospital twenty years before. It was a natural remark, coming as it did in the wake of the Braddock championship fight.

"But Mun Barrow is still here," the official answered. "Didn't you know?"

Joe Louis sent a check to cover his father's expenses, and arranged for a monthly stipend to handle his father's ongoing costs, but then went to play softball with his buddies on the team he sponsored, the Brown Bombers. He was young, intently focused on his own career, the championship belt new around his waist. His lack of curiosity about his father seemed reflected in his impassive expression in the ring. If you show no pain, perhaps you won't feel it as acutely. Joe

Louis recognized as his father Patrick Brooks, Lily's second husband, the man who had raised him — and his thirteen siblings — on Madison Avenue and Mullick Street on Detroit's east side. His natural father was a worn coin found in the last fold of a pocket.

SEARCY HOSPITAL had been a military outpost built near the junction of the Alabama and Tombigbee rivers. Set on the 31st parallel, the boundary line separating the United States and the Floridas, Fort Stoddert, as it was known, held prisoner Aaron Burr, former vice president of the United States, in 1804. Later, to escape the yellow fever that clung to the river bottoms, the settlement pushed farther into the mountains. In 1820, long after the rivers had taken the original fort, the War Department designated Mount Vernon, as the new settlement was called, an arsenal. After the Civil War it became a garrison, and in 1887 housed the most famous of its inmates, Geronimo. Apache chiefs Chihuahua and Natchez, son of Cochise, lived with their people outside the garrison in log buildings furnished by the federal government, free to go where they liked during the day, but required to be back on base by nightfall. The Apaches met trains and sold beads, and remained in Alabama until the War Department transferred them to Fort Sill, Oklahoma, in 1894.

After the Apaches' departure, the federal government turned over the reservation to the State of Alabama for public use. Initially as Mount Vernon Hospital, then renamed as Searcy, the facility followed the Kirkbridge Plan, an architectural model first embodied in the Tuscaloosa Alabama Insane Hospital, whereby a central house, or administrative building, divided male and female inmates into two wings. In 1902, 320 black patients from Tuscaloosa moved from the Alabama Insane Hospital to Mount Vernon, "a hospital designated exclusively for negroes." Not until July 1969 did government mandates desegregate Searcy Hospital, and only in 1972 did the federal courts require Alabama to improve its treatment of the mentally ill. One of the major changes stipulated that fifteen days after commitment a patient must be examined by the hospital superintendent to determine whether he or she required continued hospitalization. In Alabama during the first quarter of the twentieth century, Mun Barrow, the lowest of the economically deprived sharecropping caste, received no such evaluation.

BEFORE THE second Schmeling fight in 1938, Joe DiMaggio and Babe Ruth visited Joe Louis's training camp at Pompton Lakes, New Jersey, an hour outside of New York City. So did Jesse Owens and Bill "Bojangles" Robinson. Bojangles, who had a million minor talents in addition to his larger ones, entertained the fight crowd by lining three billiard balls in a row, then using the outside two to lift the middle ball. Holding the center ball suspended by the other two, he walked three times around the pool table. No one else could match him.

Busloads of black visitors came from Harlem, eager to meet the champ, causing the white residents of Pompton

Lakes concern. Several anonymous callers told Doc Bier, the ear-nose-and-throat physician who offered his camp to the Louis entourage, "We don't want niggers around here." The Ku Klux Klan started a letter-writing campaign to rid the town of Louis. Meanwhile, some Bundists — American Nazis — attended Louis's workout every day, mocking him and laughing. They raised their hands in a Nazi salute at his arrival and departure.

The Bundists parroted the Nazi reaction in Germany. After the first Schmeling–Louis fight, *Das Schwarze Korps*, an S.S. newspaper, announced baldly that "Schmeling's victory had saved the prestige of the white race." *Der Weltkampf*, a German magazine, said America and her allies could "not thank Schmeling enough for the victory for he checked the arrogance of the Negroes and clearly demonstrated the superiority of white intelligence." Closer to home, in the *Atlanta Journal*, O. B. Keeler called Louis a Pet Pickaninny, while Davis Walsh of the International News Service applauded the white master who had forced the "black avenger to revert to type and become again the boy who had been born in an Alabama cabin."

JOE LOUIS'S popularity after the Schmeling fight, lavish and perennial in the black community, continued to grow in white America. His mannered humility, always soft-spoken, always deferential, did not challenge the cultural status quo. He was the counter argument to Jack Johnson, who still prowled the sidelines of boxing, taunting, large, supremely confident and self-satisfied. Louis, by design and temperament, made himself easy to swallow. He refused to rise to the bait of combating a "white hope," even when Shirley Povich of the *Washington Post* wrote an article detailing former champ Jack Dempsey's plans to hold a nationwide elimination tournament to uncover a white hope. (Galento, an early Dempsey prospect, turned the tournament into a farce when he announced himself as America's "white dope.") Meanwhile, Louis kept a low profile and did not answer his detractors except in the ring. He worked tirelessly for charities. At Pompton Lakes, he put on a boxing exhibition and raised funds to purchase the village's first ambulance. He gave his time unstintingly, contributing money and rounds to milk funds and charity drives.

MONEY SWARMED him. The second Schmeling fight alone brought in approximately $350,000 at a time when a modest home cost $5,000. In four years as a professional, he had earned $1,250,000. He gave cash to anyone who asked and purchased houses, three or four, for his brothers and sisters. He engaged a chauffeur for Marva, who didn't drive, and continued to spend money as fast as it arrived. He traveled as he liked, visiting his mother often in Detroit. Each time he prepared to leave, she filled shoeboxes with chicken and sweet potato pie. The shoeboxes did not match the elegance of his outfits, nor his status as World Heavyweight Champ, so Marva shrewdly wrapped the packages in fancy paper in order that Joe could carry his mother's treats without embarrassment. Arriving home, he shouted to Marva, "Bring on the shoeboxes!"

Shopping at Saks Fifth Avenue and Billy Taub's, an exclusive tailor on 40th Street and Broadway who made clothes for Kid Chocolate, Dizzy Dean, and Babe Ruth, Marva and her husband cleaned out the stores. Marva, slim at five foot four, purchased gallons of Gardenia and Evening in Paris perfumes and carried home carloads of new outfits. Joe maintained one hundred suits in his closet, many of them purchased for close to two hundred dollars. Naturally he required hats and shoes to match, belts, suspenders, and shirts. He cared for the clothes fastidiously, frequently stopping at a tailor's to have his suit pressed while he waited behind a curtain for the work to finish. His overcoats, camel and houndstooth, hung like rich weighted curtains over his smooth frame.

With his friend, Charlie Glenn, a sportsman and prosperous Cadillac salesman, he looked into the possibility of opening a Rhumboogie Club in Detroit modeled after the club of the same name in Hollywood. He wanted to hire good jazz bands and singers, and make sure the interior came off plush and elegant, a match for the white clubs that relegated the colored community to "nigger nights" on Mondays. He eventually succeeded in 1942, participating as a silent backer and arriving in a limousine wearing an Army private's uniform on opening night, his appearance the greatest publicity a black nightclub could hope for. His brother, Pat Brooks, and his cook and former cabaret man, Bill Bottoms, worked in management. According to Helen Oakley Hines, biographer of T-Bone Walker, who played frequent engagements at the Rhumboogie, "Glenn hoped to establish the Rhumboogie as a big-league contender in the class with New York's Cotton Club and the South Side's Grand Terrace, but was too short of capital to hire an Ellington or a Hines."

IN MANY MINDS, the Schmeling–Louis rematch existed as a contest between science and nature. Schmeling represented mental acuity, intellect over brute force, Germanic precision. Louis, on the other hand, stood for animal power, a raw, nearly unconquerable vigor. Many of the comments about the champ came larded with racism. John Kieran routinely referred to Louis as Shufflin' Joe, a reference to the champ's slow, calculated forward movement, but also an allusion to shiftless plodding. Other comments insulted the champ more bluntly. Calling him an animal tamed by zookeepers, the press also referred to him as a "strange, walleyed Negro," or as something "sly and sinister and perhaps not quite human" that came out of the jungle. Mary Knight of the *Washington Post* quoted the champ loosely, turning his Alabama drawl into an excuse to mock him about his fear of swimming and water. "No, m'am, ah don't never fool wid no water. A skairt o'water. Ain't nuthin else in di' world Ah's got a fear of cep water. But Ah sho is a-feared o-dat stuff." A photographer at Louis's training camp tried to pose the champ eating watermelon. Louis refused. In the South, newsreels showing Louis training always ran at the end of the feature so it could be deleted by theater owners for white audiences.

Joe Louis was not the first fighter to be considered a missing link by virtue of his race. In the 1920s a Senegalese fighter named Louis Phal, known in the ring simply as Siki, won the light-heavyweight crown from George Carpentier — a year after Dempsey had defeated the Frenchman — at the Velodrome in Paris. On the face of it, the match seemed absurd. Siki had engaged in a few wrestling matches and one or two boxing bouts against decidedly second-raters. Carpentier took Siki lightly and scarcely trained. But the press found Siki irresistible. His French manager announced he was "determined to find a boxer who was part man and part animal." In Siki, he contended, he had found his man. Siki traveled the boulevards of Paris with an adolescent lion, scattering café crowds when he entered and propped the lion beside him. The press of the day called him an "ape man" and said he fought out of savage "atavism." When the early rounds against Carpentier went poorly, Peter Wilson, a well-known British boxing writer, described Siki as "longing to be back up a tree in Senegal."

To make the film rights more interesting and lucrative, Carpentier carried Siki through two rounds. Spectators actually preferred reading newspapers at ringside to watching the tedious match. Then Carpentier dropped Siki and stood posing for the crowd. But as Siki rose he brought his right fist with him and connected with Carpentier's jaw. What had been an easy victory for Carpentier turned into a massacre for Siki. He "went back to the caveman era" according to Wilson, and "painted the sides of [Carpentier's] face like a pillar-box with his own blood, smeared his features into a bruised, gory jelly, and generally nearly beat the life out of the dazed champion, who, a quarter of an hour earlier, had been the dapper, debonair darling of Paris."

Officials awarded the fight to Carpentier on a foul, but fortunately the decision reversed later in the evening and went to Siki on a knockout. He had won the light-heavyweight crown. Promoters arranged for him to fight Joe Beckett, the British heavyweight champion, but the Home Secretary refused to offer him a visa. (Winston Churchill, during his term as Home Secretary, had refused Jack Johnson permission to fight Billy Wells in England.) Instead Siki went to Ireland to fight Mike McTigue on St. Patrick's Day. Authorities insisted Siki be drugged and handcuffed, his handling as delicate as "some wild animal to a zoo."

Fighting an Irishman in Dublin on St. Patrick's Day, Siki lost. He traveled to the United States, where he boxed a few more years. His life ended in New York City's Hell's Kitchen, his body bleeding out in a gutter, shot, according to most conjecture, by gamblers.

IF AL JOLSON beat you at golf, he got to piss on you.

Joe Louis discovered the famous actor and singer's gambling wager on Hillcrest Golf Club in Los Angeles when he went west to take a bit part in the movie *Joe Palooka,* based on a comic strip character. When Joe Palooka's manager, Knobby Walsh, played by Leon Errol, walked in the gym, he spotted a hammy Joe Louis pounding the speed bag. "Give it up, kid, you'll never make it," Errol called, and the film crew cracked up.

Outside of Hollywood's imagination, no one could mistake the Brown Bomber for anything but the real article.

The fact that Hollywood employed him as a sight gag provides a glimpse of King Joe's notoriety. Young, handsome, a perfect body, Joe Louis was now indisputably world famous.

Joe Louis had not gone west immediately after defeating Tommy Farr in 1937. Together with Marva, he remained in New York for the World Series between the Yankees and Giants. Unknown to the spectators of that crosstown rivalry, Lou Gehrig, who had batted .351 and hit thirty-seven homers that season for the Yankees, was in the midst of playing his last meaningful series before amyotrophic lateral sclerosis robbed him of his strength, and eventually his life. Joe DiMaggio, in his second season, hit .346 with forty-six home runs and drove in an astonishing 167. The Yankees overpowered the Giants four games to one. The outcome had never been in question. The Champ watched the games avidly, his presence in the stadium cause for outbreaks of cheering and autograph signing. He enjoyed the adulation as much as the baseball.

In late October Louis traveled to Philadelphia to join his Brown Bomber softball team. Playing first base, his customary position, Louis reveled in the joy of team sport. The Bombers drew enormous crowds and people remained after the games in hopes of meeting the champ. At one game the stands collapsed under the weight of so many people. No one died, fortunately, but Louis paid for the medical bills of several injured parties. Later in the year, the team traveled to California in search of better weather. When the bus broke down, Louis called a halt to the enterprise. To do so meant taking work away from friends on the team, but he used contacts in Detroit to help them find positions at Ford.

As though the money he saved by shutting off the Brown Bombers could not rest easily with him, he backed his sister, Emmarell, in a hat shop. He also backed the Chicken Shack at 424 Vernon Street in Detroit, and opened it to a white-tie crowd. He wore a top hat and arrived in a chauffeured limousine. The restaurant ran out of chickens before the night ended, but Louis had departed by then. Like most of Louis's investments in future years, a combination of mismanagement and inattention to detail turned promise into a money sink.

In Hollywood, Arthur Stebbins, an insurance executive, invited Louis to play at the exclusive Hillcrest Golf Club in Los Angeles. Louis accepted the invitation and became the first black man to play the course. He met Jimmy Durante, Eddie Cantor, and Al Jolson, all club members. At one point Louis watched Jolson piss on a vanquished opponent. Louis accepted a wager against Jolson, risking humiliation, but beat him. He thought the entire episode was crazy, but he also said he nearly died laughing at the antics of the famous comedians. He also assumed the habit of gambling for large sums on the links. He commonly risked what would be for another man a year's salary on eighteen holes of golf.

With Marva back in Detroit, the champ strung together a series of affairs with famous movie stars. You know," he said, "there's something about women and men who can't resist each other. A big movie star would see me, the Heavyweight Champion of the World, and wonder how I am in the bed. I'd see a big beautiful movie star and wonder how she is in the bed. We would find out very easily. These were just one-night stands. But we both knew how to keep it cool. Neither of us could afford to be found out in America. . . . However, some of those one-night stands went on for weeks.

He bought Marva lavish presents to compensate for his affairs. She understood, better than anyone, the amount of attention focused on her husband, but the marriage felt strained in any case. In addition to the affairs, her husband had joined what sociologists called a cult of bachelorhood. As a result of the Depression, large sections of the male population rejected family life, finding it impossible to prove themselves as breadwinners. By some counts, 40 percent of males aged twenty-five to thirty-five remained stubbornly single. Industrialization further segregated the genders, separating them during the days at their labor, and pushing men toward recreation in pool halls, bowling alleys, firehouses, and political clubs.

And if money could not be the standard by which they would be judged, then they searched for more primal tests. Oliver Wendell Holmes Jr. described the era's attitude when he said he believed sports, like war, revealed strife to be the essence of life. "To ride boldly at what is in front of you, be it fence or enemy; to pray not for comfort but for combat; to keep the soldier's faith against the doubts of civil life, more besetting and hard to overcome than all the misgivings of the battlefields . . . to love glory more than the temptations of wallowing in ease, but to know one's final judge and only rival is oneself."

Just as boxing reflected America's movement toward mechanization and unionized labor — breaks between rounds, rest periods, a scoring system, and codified rules —

it also reflected the nation's fascination with masculine honor. Insulted, a man did not duel with guns, but might challenge his foe to a fist fight. Even in losing, a man might regain his honor. A man must accept pain without wincing, and must reject the feminization of domestic life. Boxers became the standard-bearers for men trapped in the dullness of industrialized America, men whose increasing leisure time gave them opportunities to live vicariously through the exploits of their heroes.

In short, if the Heavyweight Champion of the World looked to play, he found no shortage of willing companions, men whose ambivalence about domestic life matched Louis's own. The champ remained surrounded by men, except for his sexual excursions, and he returned quickly to the world of men after these affairs. Julian Black and John Roxborough, his managers, and Chappie Blackburn, his trainer, formed a ring of masculine influence around him that trumped any commitment to Marva or family life. His secretary, Russell Cowans, a former journalist for the *Detroit Chronicle* who helped the champ answer mail and coached him on social niceties, left him at the start of 1938, fatigued by travel and by the unrelenting maleness of the boxing world.

But Joe Louis thrived in such a world. Constantly in motion, constantly away, he remained happiest at the crowded training table in Pompton Lakes, men circling him, his status unrivaled and entirely provable.

AT THE END of 1938, Gus Greenlee, John Henry Lewis's manager, secured a date for a bout with Joe

Louis. It was a plum for John Henry Lewis, who stood at the end of his long career. His great-great uncle, Tom Molineaux, had been a Virginia slave famous for his boxing skills. John Henry Lewis had fought over one hundred matches since turning pro in 1931 and had been the first American-born black man to win the light-heavyweight crown. He had lost three times to Slapsie Maxie Rosenbloom, but had split decisions with James Braddock, former heavyweight champ. Known for his defense, he was a consummate long-range boxer, a flashy otter, a fighter with an uncanny ability to dodge in and out of harm's way. And he was black. His proposed fight with Tony Galento, after much ballyhoo, had fallen through due to Galento's pneumonia. He needed a date.

Mike Jacobs, Louis's longtime manager, did not like the match for the champ. Lewis, although a sturdy veteran and the Light-Heavyweight Champion of the World, could do little but detract from Joe Louis's luster. A man boxing down in a weight class fights against his opponent and the inevitable public opinion that the larger man should win in any case. On the other hand, if Louis lost, or appeared clumsy in the process of winning, he would be humiliated, his career tarnished. To sour the match further, Mike Jacobs did not like the pairing of two black men as a box-office draw. Both men were supported by black managers and trainers; both men trailed black entourages after them. Jacobs was above all an astute businessman. Despite the black press's enthusiastic support of the proposed match, and despite the comparative skill of the boxers, he feared matching the popular Louis with another black fighter might cause white America to stay away.

But Joe Louis wanted the fight. He understood better than anyone how difficult John Henry Lewis's career as a black fighter had been. He also understood that Lewis would not have many more fights. A rumor followed Lewis — subsequently the cause for the end of his career — that he could not see laterally out of his left eye. Such an injury, if confirmed, spelled the end of Lewis's fighting days. Confident that he could beat the lighter man, Louis wanted to send his friend and colleague into retirement with a solid payday. He wrote about the arrangement in his autobiography.

> My mind was together; I was going to fight John Henry Lewis — the first time in modern boxing history two black men would meet for a heavyweight championship fight. I hear tell that during slavery days black slaves always were fighting in the ring for their masters, and there were big bets. Well, the white man is clever. When they finally realized that all that money was going down, the white man replaced the black man in the ring. Now I felt really good. Here I was, a black man, going to fight another black man, and us blacks are on the money side this time. Jesus Christ, blacks may make it yet!

To Mike Jacobs's delight, the fight between the two black boxers received the full treatment by the press and public. Ring historians uncovered that twenty-six years had passed since two black men had fought for the championship. Jack Johnson and Jim Johnson, in what some called an exhibition and others contended was a match, squared off in Paris in

1913. Never in America had two black men faced each other for the heavyweight title. The public also voted its interest by filling Madison Square Garden to capacity. Eighteen thousand tickets sold. It marked the fourth time the champ had sold out the Garden and the fourth time the gate had grossed more than one hundred thousand dollars. Regardless of his opponent, Joe Louis had become a certifiable attraction.

In the end, only the fight disappointed. Although experts held out hope that Lewis's superb ring craft might balance the scales, Louis proved too strong and quick for the light-heavyweight. The odds — 6 to 1 in favor of Louis — proved too optimistic for Lewis. Outweighing the lighter man by twenty pounds, the Brown Bomber overwhelmed Lewis, knocking him down three times in the first round. The assault began with a right cross, after which, according to Arch Ward of the *Chicago Tribune*, "John Henry staggered around the ring on putty props, a wounded, bleeding man, carrying the cross of his own great courage, a gallant soldier of the ring, badly whipped but refusing to surrender."

The hope that Lewis might hold off Louis with boxing skills was abandoned twenty seconds into the hostilities. Lewis returned one punch that grazed the larger man's shoulder, but Louis, by all accounts, never took a single step backward. He pumped a left and right into John Henry's stomach, then lifted a right to the jaw that sent the challenger through the lower strand of ropes.

Referee Arthur Donovan untangled the lighter man, who stood swaying on cellophane legs, awaiting the coup de grâce. Fans shouted for the referee to stop the bout, but Louis ended it before anyone could intercede. He rifled a right to John

Henry's chin. John Henry, who had never been knocked out, took distance into his eyes and fell flat on his back. When he climbed to his feet again, Donovan lifted the Brown Bomber's arm in victory. For the first time in heavyweight history, a champion had won two consecutive matches in the initial round — first against Schmeling, now Lewis.

The fight shocked many observers, not merely by the one-sidedness of the contest, but by the sheer violence expressed in Louis's punches. Arch Ward of the *Tribune* called it "one of those magnificent spectacles of brutality." Several writers likened Louis to a panther, a sublime animal nearly unconquerable by more human adversaries. One writer compared his flurry of punches to a typhoon. Clearly Joe Louis had become the most formidable heavyweight fighting. In his mid-twenties, at the peak of his prowess, he punched squarely from his prime.

Fifteen minutes after the bout concluded, John Henry Lewis still had the knockdown count wrong. Claiming that the referee shouldn't have stopped it, he put in a hopeless bid for a rematch. "I thought there was a rule in this State to the effect that a fighter must be knocked down three times before the bout is stopped on him, and I was only down twice."

When his manager, Gus Greenlee, pointed out that he had been down three times, John Henry Lewis merely nodded. The next day Lewis asked for a return match again, but no one took the possibility seriously. Before he could fight again, doctors examined his eye and declared him unfit for pugilism. He left the ring a loser, but a fighter with the distinction of going up against the heavyweight champ. His take for the match was $11,741.17.

8

THE MOST EFFECTIVE punch is a short punch. It is straight and level and creates a momentary plank between the shoulder of one boxer and the chin of the other. The logical completion, though never achieved, is somewhere in the gelled glue of the brain, the nutty center of the skull. The hitter's fist grips into a tight ball and the impact of the punch crunches the knuckles down, sends a vibration into the forearm and deep into the elbow. If the receiver is moving forward, as Tony Galento always did, then the punch becomes a cracking smack too painful at first to comprehend. The receiver impales himself on his opponent's fist, so to speak, and absorbs the additional thrust the two objects create in collision.

DESPITE GALENTO'S scoring a knockdown of the Bomber in round three, and despite the jubilation they felt, his corner saw trouble. Sitting on the stool, his arms wide at the elbows but his wrists propped demurely on his knees, Tony appeared a mash of blood and drool and water. He sweated copiously, his brow and chest a river, his gloves two dark deltas of sentiment and gunk. Bimstein worked over him, trying to close the cut above his boy's right eye, but that work required more time than the minute of rest he had at his disposal. He pinched the cut hard, ministered to the other gouges and punctures that he noted on his quick inspection. It hardly mattered now if Referee Donovan swung by to check on the bloody gashes, because no one, not even Commissioner Phelan himself, could halt a fight after the challenger had knocked down the reigning champ. Nevertheless, Bimstein understood a moment of desperation had arrived. The fight could not continue much longer. Louis had both hands landing at will, and the Brown Bomber had a ferocious kick, his jab "an abrupt piece of punctuation," as one writer described it. Galento had to land something soon, something even more devastating than his knockdown punch, or he would sink under Louis's pressure.

With twenty seconds to go, Bimstein began to clear. Joe Jacobs, screaming and following his hands out of the ring, squawked that Tony had to move, to crouch, to hit the bastard. Jimmy Frain went about the orderly custodial business, mopping his corner with a free towel, smearing blood and water and spit together in a white curl of cotton he preferred not to examine. At ten seconds the ring emptied except for the two contestants. Each man had been down once. Above them smoke and evening mist collected in the light.

* * *

THE BELL RANG for the fourth. Galento rose slowly and made his way toward the center of the ring, the enthusiasm he might have felt after scoring a knockdown muted and surrendered. His corner shouted for him to crouch, to become a leaden grasshopper with V-shaped arms tucked at his side, but fatigue had robbed him of his ability to follow commands. He walked upright, swaggering still, his hands at his waistline, his face jutting forward. He had put Louis down the round before, and though he comprehended his own exhaustion, he clapped his gloves together to demonstrate his readiness. His gloves glistened and dripped with his sweat.

Almost immediately Louis began pelting Galento, hitting him with solid punches while Galento's hooks scraped air. Louis's combinations appeared to arrive the instant Galento hatched the inspiration for his own next punch, a brutal interruption of any tactic Tony could conceive. Whatever plans Louis had contemplated to carry Tony in order to beat him, to humiliate him, had been abandoned after the third-round knockdown. Louis now demonstrated his mastery. He rotated slowly to the left, stirred by Galento's left hook, but no longer particularly afraid of it. His punches came in twos, then threes. Twice Galento stood before him, his arms covering his body and head, his nakedness humbling. Galento had run out of gas. It is a boxing equation that the more one is hit, the more one will be open to being hit. In the newsreel afterward, people counted Louis landing thirty clean punches in the fourth round, twenty-eight of them to Galento's head.

* * *

TO WATCH now, as the fans from ringside did, forced a person to turn his body, to pretend interest elsewhere, as if by turning one could shuck the responsibility for what had occurred. One was not a barbarian, after all. One did not relish another man's anguish, and so it was bad form to appear too interested, too lustful, to lean forward and watch with any emotion approaching pleasure or keen appetite. But, of course, the impending devastation remained the core of the experience, so no one turned away entirely, no one chanced missing the final blow. They sent empathy to the Orange bartender; they sent understanding. Above all, they forgave him. They forgave him his weakness, his inability to defeat the great Joe Louis, and they forgave his final clumsiness.

By a trick of imagination they pretended to themselves that they would never wish this, not this particular thing, on a good fellow like Tony. The lie was revealed, however, by their unwillingness to look away. They wanted his last end. They wanted him beaten, skillfully crushed, his head knocked back on his shoulders. They wanted him to accept his beating as a wage for the wage he received, to honor the bargain, and they wanted, as much as anything, to be present when Louis administered the coup de grâce. Had the Bomber stopped and asked, as he might have of Roman emperors, to kill or to spare a life, the answer would have been unanimous. Don't kill him, they would have said, but don't spare him a single blow.

* * *

THE PHOTOGRAPHERS at ringside pressed closer, feeling the ending near. The men wore suit jackets and hats and carried flash attachments the size of hand mirrors on top of their apparatuses. They propped their cameras on the apron of the ring, just outside the vertical line of ropes. They pointed their cameras up at an angle, and let the fighters swing into frame, disappear, return. Chance always played a role in getting the best shot, and each photographer tried to capture what he could as background, relying on luck to bring him the defining photo. The camera flashes went off like small explosions, and seen against the darkness of the sky, the boxers seemed to fight in a lightning storm, their arms and faces frozen in a strobe effect. The photographers tried to frame meaning into the whirl of arms, legs, sweat. Their work would appear in the next day's newspapers, on the front of the *New York Times*, in *Life Magazine*, in *Time*. Luck might turn their assignment into art, but they could not aim for anything too refined. They lifted their eye from the viewfinder, replaced it, returned it. They resembled prairie dogs lifting out of their holes to see what approached. Above them the men fought and twirled around the ring, an object of angles and lighting and depth to the men below them. Everywhere flashes of aluminum burned bright and slowly faded.

A MINUTE, or thirty punches, into the round, Louis hit Galento with a perfect right to the chin, a blow so devastating it knocked Galento sideways. Tony's head turned as if listening to a yell somewhere distant, and he could not bring his attention back from where Louis had sent it. Louis followed up smoothly, nearly routinely, smelling the end, encountering no resistance. He hit Tony with a left, a right, another right. Galento went back against the ropes and his hands dropped. He lost all secondary dimensionality; he had become a paper cutout, a drying sheet on a clothesline that Louis hit twice, three times, his hand moving faster than the eye could follow. A brittle senility entered Galento's movement and expression, and Donovan, studying the challenger, waffled for the smallest instant. Then Louis hit Galento again, sending him bouncing on the rope, and Donovan stepped in between, a shade uncertain, until Tony stepped sideways and fell. It appeared a misstep, a man going off a loading dock, but Galento slid to one knee.

Donovan embraced him, held him and tried to lift, while Louis, respectful now, stepped away. "Come up and get him," Donovan said softly to Galento's corner.

The moment, photographed and published in *Life* on July 10, 1939, remains flawless in its composition. In the forefront Galento kneels on his left leg, his ear against Donovan's heart, his eyes swollen shut. Donovan's face, stern, his attention elsewhere, exhibits pity and sadness not for Galento alone, but for effort and loss in human endeavor. Louis, peering over Donovan's right shoulder, is momentarily guilty, his hands murderous, his complicity in such humiliation as purely human as the suffering before him.

* * *

FOR A MOMENT Donovan's intention did not come completely clear to everyone in the stadium. Far up in the bleachers, back where the two pugilists appeared as small as robins pecking at the same grub, nothing would satisfy but a knockout. Those beside the ring, those who had seen the pulverizing force of the punches, did not for a moment doubt Donovan had interceded to end the fight.

Fans saw Louis back away, his face expressionless, his corner men rising to receive him. The corner men moved carefully — like all black men under the scrutiny of beaten white men — with the quiet authority of funeral directors. Inside their hearts they felt the satisfaction of a successful defense, but they could not show it. Instead they busied themselves with the everyday labor of buckets and sponges, deflecting the pleasure of accomplishment into the mundane. Later, they knew, they could celebrate. Later they could taste the glory with all its succulence. Perhaps their pleasure would be heightened by the delay. For the moment, however, they accepted the bomber calmly. Chappie Blackburn nodded his approval and rubbed a towel over the champ's face. They were relieved to be finished with the fat little Italian. Fuck him and all his nigger talk. Fuck him with his joking and jiving, his stupid phone calls late at night. Maybe now he would understand what was what. But he was a tough customer, they granted, and they were glad to put him in the record book.

* * *

THE GALENTOS — Tony's brother, Russell, and his wife, Mildred, and Tony's own wife, Mary — and the cousins, the siblings, the vibrant mass of Orange citizens, all stood as soon as Donovan stopped the fight, but slowly realized they had no place to go. Tony remained here, in front of them, and to move away, to give in to the desire to flee, would accomplish nothing. It was over.

Around them people shouted and screamed, but those removed by social distance or blood did not reach over to console the relatives. Instead they came to their defense, stepping in to assume a portion of the loss. They directed everything outward, angry, still wanting somehow to salvage what had become lost to them forever in a single boxing round. To lose a fight of this proportion, to come so close, left nothing to say. Some lit new cigarettes. Others gestured, insulting Louis and his retinue, wanting somehow to take the fight onto their own shoulders, refusing to admit the Bomber had proved the better man.

Some had lost money and could not escape a quick calculation; others had lost bets of pride, boasts of Italian superiority. Now it had all been shoved back in their faces and they looked to avert their eyes, to see something other than Tony's bleeding carcass being lugged to his stool. They looked, too, for a cheat in the victory. Something had given Louis an edge. They could not discern it now, not at that instant of triumph for the darkie, but something had to be crooked. If nothing else, they felt the indignation of a band of people made to wait too long. If Tony had been younger, they thought, if Tony had not nearly died of pneumonia, if the fucking Jew managers hadn't dicked around and strung everything out for the extra years, then Tony might be sitting up while Joe Louis dragged his heels back to the stool. Things could have been different, they knew, but now it had all been spoiled and they felt that early pain in their gut and in the sinking clutch of their hearts when they looked at poor Tony.

OUTSIDE THE stadium the police horses woke from their easy dozes and stepped a little to get their blood moving, their hooves clopping on the cobblestones. Suddenly the stadium took on a different air. The fight had ended. You could feel it closing down. The cheers and roaring changed to a funnel of noise moving outward. The first few fans burst out of the barrel-arched doorways, flooded into the street, still talking and shouting. Most smoked cigarettes. Most shouted answers to questions from the vendors, from the policemen, from anyone who wanted to lift the burden of such a spectacle from them.

The Brown Bomber, they said. Too good. In no time their numbers tripled, doubled again, clogged the streets as they hurried to get to the subway.

Viewed from above, the scene might have been the detonation of a bomb, the broadcast of a handful of grain, because the instant the fight ended people began moving out and away. Now, with the fight under their belts, they were experts heading home with the report of something miraculous. A hell of a fight. Better than anyone had anticipated.

They swarmed up the metal stairs to the subways, their shoes making loud scuffling sounds, the trains grinding to stops beside them. To be the first, now, to deliver the story firsthand, that was tasting life twice. It would become their story to tell, a marvel they alone had witnessed. In the office, around the kitchen table, at the job site, in the bars, they could bank on the story to hold interest. They saw the Galento–Louis fight. They had been there and they could hardly believe their good fortune at seeing such a bout.

9

A TRAVELING SALESMAN, Robert Amkenbrand, sixty-five, of Philadelphia, listened to the Louis–Galento fight at the Berkshire Hotel at 321 North Street in Pittsfield, Massachusetts. People near him said he seemed extremely agitated as he listened, and when the announcer described Louis's hand held up in victory, Amkenbrand slumped over and died. The news article failed to establish if Amkenbrand had been rooting for Galento or the Brown Bomber.

A Montclair, New Jersey, woman, Mrs. Malinda Williams, forty-six, died after collapsing when Galento knocked Louis down. I. J. Amo, fifty-four, of Plainfield passed away at the home of his niece, Mrs. Howard Thompson, in Westfield, New Jersey, as the family listened to the fight. He died fifteen minutes after his initial collapse despite efforts to revive him.

The Associated Press reported that others stricken were: John M. Chirrick, seventy-two, of Mitchell, Nebraska; James Mason, sixty-two, and Santa Rosa, sixty-nine, both of Philadelphia.

ON WHAT was labeled Minnesota Day at the World's Fair, and was also coincidentally the evening of the Louis–Galento fight, Maria Sarkipato, reputed to be the only girl hunting and fishing guide in the country, demonstrated the proper technique for portaging a canoe. Earlier in the week she had traveled on a special fishing trip to land toque and walleye that she intended to present to Mayor LaGuardia. The canoe, observers swore, weighed over one hundred pounds. Sarkipato carried it on her shoulders, the bow and stern pointed forward and back like an admiral's cap. She carried it to and fro, pretending to place it in a stream, ready it, then begin the portage again.

DWELLERS IN the Negro section of Orange hailed the Louis victory with loud talk and laughter, but that was about all. Police reported minor difficulty in keeping the streets clear. Four youths were arrested and charged with disorderly conduct. Judge McHugh at the night court fined them each one dollar and sent them home.

In Newark, tension, suppressed during the fight, broke out when the ring announcer declared Louis "winna and still champeen." Police radio dispatchers at Newark headquarters remained idle until that moment. The police made no arrests.

In Harlem, in Chicago, in other black enclaves around the country, the celebrations did not rise to the pitch established after Louis's victories over Carnera or Schmeling. The black population knew Joe Louis as a working champ now, a man who could only bring excitement by failure, and they did not expect him to fail for a long time. Galento had been game, they granted, but he had not been in Louis's class. It made little sense to celebrate the efficiency demonstrated by the Sepia Socker. Pride, yes, they felt pride, but it no longer came mixed with surprise and overwhelming jubilation. It did not require demonstrations, loud parades, people throwing noisy gear off apartment roofs. To be a champ Louis had to defeat challengers like Two Ton Tony Galento routinely, and the wrong kind of celebration at this point might have betrayed doubt.

TONY GALENTO, meanwhile, sat in the center of a police ring in his corner while Dr. William Walker attempted to resuscitate him. The next day Dr. Walker would contend, in answer to some caviling from New Jersey that the fight had been stopped too soon, that Art Donovan had stopped the fight at precisely the correct moment. More blows, Walker said, might have resulted in profound injury. Even with Donovan's well-timed interruption, Two Ton Tony could not move or respond to questions Walker put to him. His lips had split like cheap paneling and his nose had been beaten flat against his face. Blood dripped from several cuts, pouring a crimson rope onto the pale canvas when he stirred. Bimstein and Frain massaged him, trying to combat his numbness. The crowd at ringside watched the men's expressions to gauge Tony's recovery. Dr. Walker bathed Galento's face and spoke to him, calling him back to the stadium, waving smelling salts under his nose. Five minutes after the fight had ended, Tony Galento regained consciousness.

LOUIS REMAINED in the ring until Galento had recovered sufficiently to stand. He floated in the crowd of men, his white terrycloth robe brilliant next to the drabness of the dark-suits and the police bluecoats. Ring announcer Harry Ballow gave the tell, speaking forcefully into a microphone brought to him by a member of Mike Jacobs's production crew. At 2:29 of the fourth round, by technical knockout, still Heavyweight Champion of the World, Joe Louis.

At the conclusion of the announcement, Louis raised his right hand and waved his glove. Fans nodded. This made sense. They lingered near their seats, still thrilled, their pleasure in the aftermath nearly as profound as the stimulation of the fight itself. Everywhere men talked, compared observations, confessed they did not think Louis could be beaten. Others interjected that Galento had hit him, after all, you had to give him that, geez what a left the guy has, really. Fight people conjectured about a return bout. Louis would be crazy, they concluded, to risk it against Galento again, but they admitted it seemed a bankable fight. Several people pointed out that the bout would have drawn better, substantially better, if they had moved it to Philadelphia, where Tony's name proved a license to print money. Louis had to fight Lou Nova sooner or later, and Nova, they guessed, had as good a chance as anyone to defeat Louis. Big, handsome kid from California. A vegetarian. Practiced yoga or something. Still green, but a comer. Good money match.

FINALLY, WITH men supporting him, Tony Galento stood. The police ring closed to shield him from view. His legs came under him gradually. Nearby fans began to clap, but they were too scattered to catch fire. A few Orange boosters shouted good wishes, cheered him, told him he had been stopped too early by Referee Donovan. Tony raised a hand, waved, his face a blue bulb. A yoke of blood covered his shoulders and chest. His managers pulled the ropes apart like a bowstring, and Tony stepped onto the apron of the ring and descended the stairs to the stadium grass.

Suddenly the glamour of the moment gave way to the pale truth of the situation: a beaten man, his brain a kettle of bees, walked with assistance through abandoned chairs, past vendors pausing to look, past the scattered imprint of fans turning to leave. He looked old. He look frail and tentative, his balance giving way, after all, for the first time in his life. Watching him, the fans noted the moment when an athlete is reduced to a Little Leaguer, to another sweaty fellow looking for victory, to a human instead of lauded combatant in an outsized arena. He had become flesh and blood to those fans around him, and they pushed back and let him pass, showed solicitousness over his condition that, a few minutes before, had been shattered in their name.

It's impossible to know the details he noticed on the walk to the locker room. Perhaps he noticed the luxuriousness of the summer grass, trampled in places by fans, or noticed the detritus of cigar butts and paper cups. Certainly people called to him, reached forward between policemen to slap his back. Perhaps his eyes cleared enough to see the faces behind the people, but it is equally likely he could see only moderately well, his eyelid jammed with blood and liquid, his gaze an animal's glance of lidded eyes and back-tilted head.

Smoke trailed his small group as it pushed toward the locker room, and reporters, doubtless, shouted questions. Maybe he felt the evening coolness strike his chest, or felt, at last, the throbbing ache of his hands. With each step his head cleared a little more, and he followed the swarm of his supporters, their bodies a prow pushing people away. Above him lights from the stadium pulled a thousand insects toward their brightness, and bats cut the beams as they passed back and forth to feed.

FOR SPENDING eleven-plus minutes in the ring battling the Brown Bomber, Tony Galento had earned $42,141.37, the standard contender percentage of the $288,303.68 gross receipts. Joe Louis, whose skin showed no signs of being in a fight, whose body had not swollen under Galento's blows, carried $96,323.12 back to the locker room. The fee Louis received fell short of Mae West's $339,166 salary, or Bing Crosby's $192,948, but it was eighty times the average annual salary of an American schoolteacher, who received $1,200 for a year's work with children. As lucrative as the evening had been for Louis, it did not match the $150,000 per minute he had earned against Max Schmeling in their second bout. For his three paydays in 1939, Louis grossed $273,986.

IN THE LOCKER room Galento sat quietly on the rubdown table and let Dr. Walker tend to him. He still had not regained an alert consciousness. The beating he endured had crushed his face, opened wide gaps that required stitches. In the excitement of the aftermath, in the slow, burgeoning understanding, Galento's accomplishment began to take form, though Galento himself felt unmoved. He had lost the championship. The ache of his legs, his fists, his battered face, could not obscure the knowledge that he had rocked the champ in the first, put him down in the third, and had not finished him.

The moist locker room, the skid of shoes on the cement floor, and the occasional whack of a rolled-up program hitting the arm of a nearby spectator drifted to Tony as he assessed his body. Friends passed by, congratulated him, told him next time. Cops protected the door, letting people in only if approved by Frain or Jacobs or Bimstein. Tony nodded at his well-wishers, his head down. Despite his image as a clown, as a buffoon with a cigar and a growler of beer always at hand, he had dedicated himself to beating Louis. True, he had not trained as assiduously as he should have, and he had clowned and aped so much that at times he felt carried away by the ballyhoo, but his heart had known another truth. He had meant to win; he had hit the champ with everything he had and still the champ had won.

Every boxer must face retirement, and the ultimate betrayal of his body, but Galento had endured the doubly cruel fate of tasting victory before losing it. He believed he could have beaten Louis, that he would one day beat the Bomber, and that belief propelled him off the table, sent him slowly walking back to the showers. Like many athletes, he walked on the outside of his feet, his ursine bulk rounded and blunt. He disappeared into the stalls, the hiss of water and steam covering him for a moment and leaving him alone to rediscover his body. Without meaning to, the people waiting for him lowered their voices, conferred quietly. They desired to show respect for their champion, and to lower their voice in the company of such pain seemed merely natural.

IN THE HALLWAY outside of the locker room, Joe Louis slipped his fedora back on his head, tilting it front to back the way a man seals a coffee can, the brim creating a smooth line that bisected his forehead. A handsome man, he had dressed with casual elegance for the fight. Now he stood in front of cameras and microphones again, aware, as always, of John Roxborough's injunction to show no pleasure at the defeat of a white opponent.

Tony Galento was game, he said in answer to the inevitable questions. As tough a man as he had ever fought. He could take a punch, the Bomber said, better than anyone else he could bring to mind. Good and game, he repeated. To one reporter who asked whether Tony Galento had hurt him, Louis replied, "Well, he knocked me down." Then he touched the brim of his hat, smiled, and the cameras let him go. This night, despite his capable defense of the championship, he was not the story.

The newsreel released the following day carried Louis's assessment of Galento. Only a week or two later did Louis clarify that the knockdown in the third, the subject of everyone's congratulations for Galento, had been nothing more than a flash. It had not hurt him; it had merely caught him off balance. A flash knockdown, he called it. Fight fans debated the truth of that statement for the next half century.

But on this June night, Louis left the stadium with his entourage in tow. Still champeen. Still the hardest man in the world. No one doubted he had been in a fight, but he had won cleanly and convincingly. His next fight, against Bob Pastor, stood a comfortable three months away. Plenty of time. Plenty of everything. Years remained before he would lose or suffer the humiliation of being slugged through the ropes by a young Marciano, an Italian kid with a background not unlike Galento's. On that night the nation — and even Marciano — would weep at the inevitability of time, and the hubris of all men too proud to ignore the knock on their own door.

But this night black kids screamed and yelled his name as he climbed into his automobile after shaking hands with well-wishers. King Joe. Or simply Joe. The kids climbed on the bases of streetlamps and onto mailboxes to see him. They felt the excitement in their legs and in their guts. The mounted police kept the crowd back until the car gained speed and shed the adoring fans. Joe Louis disappeared into the Bronx, his body unused, his entourage, in the privacy of the car, starting to release its delight at last.

THE NIGHT remained humid. The sea breeze that had begun at midday slowly reversed, but the land did not relinquish the heat entirely. Warmth still pushed up from the macadam and from the pale sidewalks, and even the gray girders of Yankee Stadium retained part of the day's sunlight. Vendors outside the stadium circled or tried to catch the crowd as it continued to sift into the subways. The mounted police plodded slowly around the perimeter of the stadium portals, making sure people moved along. Now and then a subway clattered on the elevated tracks above them, and the lights of the trains flickered like a coil of film slowly unraveling before light.

The quickest members of the crowd, and the hard-drinking sportswriters, scurried to Jack Dempsey's restaurant on 40th Street and Eighth Avenue. Though he had once managed Tony Galento, Dempsey did not attend the fight. He had predicted an easy Louis victory from Louisville, where he had traveled to referee a wrestling match. He also talked about managing Tony Galento. "I used to have him five years ago. He was better then than he is now. He is wide open. What if he should by some chance hit Louis? Joe is game. He can get up off the floor."

Dempsey had gone on to predict Galento would not be standing after the first round. He called anyone who bought a ticket for the fight a sucker. The comment sent Joe Jacobs popping off the ground. He challenged Dempsey to wager fifteen thousand dollars at even money that Galento would be on his feet for round two and a lot more besides. Tony merely shrugged, refusing the bait. "Dempsey?" he asked. "Who's he? He's just another guy in the liquor business like me."

On this night it paid for Dempsey to be in the liquor business, because his bar filled with the after-fight crowd. The writers ordered drinks and food and tried to reconstruct what they had seen. Some claimed Louis had been hurt in the third; others said the big punch for Galento came in the first. Either way, Galento deserved a tip of the cap. With cigars and cigarettes pushing smoke across the bar, the men drank and talked and remembered the fight collectively. It would be their telling of the fight that people remembered, and already, as they began to shape the idea of what had occurred, the lead had to center on Two Ton Tony Galento.

WHEN THE STORIES these men wrote came out the next day, they labeled Tony "the clown who fought like a hero." Papers across the country called him gallant, a loser who fought courageously.

"The suckers who paid for their tickets had no right to expect to get so much for their money. The promoter, the boxing commission, the manager, the press just made this one up," wrote Bruce Bliven Jr. in an articled titled "Humpty Dumpty Had a Great Fall":

They made up a fighter, they made up a fight, and a few more than 35,000 paid to see their brainchild. Everybody knew it was phony but the guy himself, the Two Ton Tony Galento. Out of the words and pictures emerged their fantastic, imaginary fighter — Two Ton Tony Galento of Orange, New Jersey, fat and bald, who trained on beer and cigars and late hours behind the bar of his saloon and said Joe Louis was a bum. They said he couldn't speak, they wanted him fingerprinted and they speculated about his fighting a gorilla. Then they put him in a ring in the Yankee Stadium against the Champion, just for the fun of it and the curiosity money it would draw, forgetting of course that their made-up fighter was a man with a heart.

In the *New York Times* John Lardner wrote:

Tony Galento, whose heart is nearly as big as his vast, round fur-bearing chest, created the best heavyweight championship fight since the Dempsey–Firpo thing when he stood up to Joe Louis and threw wild left hooks till his time, strength and consciousness ran out in the fourth round. Referee Arthur Donovan stopped the carnage when Galento slid to his hips and then fell back on his spine under a salvo of 28 rights and lefts. Galento's face was a scarlet circle, and he had to be dragged to his corner. But before they lugged him away, the fat little barkeep brought 35,000 hearts into 35,000 throats with his valor and crazy strength.

"All the world loves a winner," Ted Carroll wrote in *The Ring,* the magazine dedicated to boxing. "But it has been shown time and again that a gallant loser is acclaimed by all. Many a winner's fame is but momentary, while the name of many a gallant loser never will be forgotten."

Galento's stock had risen overnight. In the days that followed the bout, other writers toasted him, some even apologizing for not taking his challenge seriously. A few sportswriters used his near success with Louis to denigrate the champ, calling the Brown Bomber overrated. In a more thoughtful appreciation of Galento, John J. Hall, writing in a column called *From Where We Sit,* mused about what might have happened if Two Ton had received better handling at an earlier stage of his career.

> Tony Galento will never beat the Brown Bomber. And yet, slashed and torn and battered as he was in that gory battle above the ball park's second base over which another Italian, Tony Lazzeri, had ruled for so many years, the bulky man from Orange showed sufficient to send thoughts racing back to what might have been if only the Galento of seven years ago had been the serious fighter he was last week at Summit [Madame Bey's].

The theme played over and over in papers and on radio broadcasts. It was an American theme about overlooked champions, men and women who, under different circumstances, better handling, smarter moves, might have achieved something memorable. Coming as it did at the bitter end of the Depression, readers and listeners understood it intuitively. Perhaps it was a fantasy, because Tony, like others, had lived his fate and made his own poor calculations. And maybe only his left hand had brought the matter to anyone's attention, a lucky blow, perhaps, or the diminished greatness of a fighter whose heart surprised all who counted him out beforehand. One punch had slipped through the Brown Bomber's superior artfulness, and Tony Galento followed it into the darkness he nearly brought to his opponent, and became in that instant another near success. You could not blame such a man, because in your own life you understood his failure better than you understood Louis's triumph. And the next morning over coffee, in a bar facing a beer, on the subway sagging with the rock of the car over the rails, on the Jersey ferry with your paper tucked into the clamp of your hand, you shook your head as you read the fight account, and found yourself smiling, because Tony had been swinging leather, by God, and he had been swinging it all his life. And Joe Louis, despite his grace and fluid skills, had forgotten to duck in time, and some great justice resided there, but asked to name it, you couldn't bring it to your lips.

10

LIKE MANY FIGHTERS of his day, Tony wrestled when he retired. Under the management of New Jersey promoter Willie Gilzenberg he toured the country, wrestling and putting on shows. His wrestling moniker, naturally, was Two Ton Tony Galento, and his secret weapon — all wrestlers have secret weapons — was his "left hook that nearly pried the crown off Joe Louis's head." Caught in a pinch, facing defeat, he plied the left hook and rallied himself to victory. Sometimes he refereed a match when, against his peaceful nature, he could not help being drawn into the fracas.

He faced Primo Carnera in Newark and battled the giant to a draw. Like Galento, Carnera was an Italian. An immigrant, a boxer of mediocre skill, he was the first Italian boxer to win the heavyweight belt. Bigger than any heavyweight who fought for the championship — with the possible exception of Jess Willard — he stood six-foot-six and weighed 260 pounds. His muscles, impossibly defined on a man of such size, stretched across his frame until his ribs became zippers of bone. His face, battered and slightly ill-formed from gigantism, appeared too mild for a boxer's trade. Used and propped up by gamblers, his life formed the basis of Humphrey Bogart's last film, *The Harder They Fall.* He towered over Two Ton Tony, but Galento, in inimitable wrestling style, managed to thwart the bigger man. Although they grappled for the requisite five minutes, neither gained an advantage. The match resulted in a draw, but it was one, the public address system assured the crowd, that could be rejoined in Pittsburgh the following week.

Inspired by the match, a fan wrote a polka for Galento that sometimes played as Tony rumbled into the ring:

> Heigh-Ho Tony, he's champion wrestler,
> number one!
> Heigh-Ho, Tony, see how he's got them
> on the run.
> Heigh-Ho, Tony, he will give the crowd a thrill!
> First a left, and a right, then a tackle and a bite,
> until his foe is lying still!

PERHAPS the highlight of Galento's wrestling career came in Seattle, when a promoter arranged for him to take on an octopus. The promoter made the pitch to Willie Gilzenberg. The two men had been drinking at a bar and hatched the idea after several rounds. After several more rounds, during which time they petted the notion until it came alive and took on a life of its own, they grew close to setting terms. Unwilling to accept such a match, however inspired, without Tony's consent, Gilzenberg went upstairs to Galento's room, woke his client, and asked him if he minded wrestling an octopus. Galento, barely awake, said it would be no problem.

The next day he went to the wrestling arena, where the Seattle promoter had erected an enormous aquarium. An octopus of significant size, with a head like a deflated basketball, floated in the center of the great tank. When Tony realized he was scheduled to dive down to face the octopus, he expressed genuine terror. But the crowd filled the arena and Gilzenberg, nursing his charge, stood behind Tony as he climbed the ladder. Tony entered the water gingerly, whereupon the octopus squirted its defensive ink. Accounts vary about what happened next. Some say Tony bit the octopus and others say the octopus bit Tony. Another account has it that Tony strangled it "by mistake." For the fans in the arena, it was all but impossible to see due to the copious amounts of ink. Tony came out of the tank like a breaching whale and nearly crushed Gilzenberg in his eagerness to get down the ladder.

At the Laurel Garden in Newark Tony boxed Teddy, a 550-pound Russian bear. Fighting in a cage to protect innocent audience members, the bear landed several hard punches to the chin and knocked Tony down for a five-count. In the next round Tony went loopy for a six-count, while the animal trainers prepared to drive off the bear if it became too agitated. Eventually the fight was halted. Teddy, according to most judges, won the contest.

Tony raced swimming champion Buster Crabbe in a Patterson aqua-show, boxed a kangaroo on the boardwalk in Atlantic City, and rode a bucking bronco in Albany. He went on the radio with Charlie McCarthy and batted against Cleveland ace Bob Feller. A movie studio contacted him to "demonstrate how an American boxer can lick a Jap jujitsu artist." The film was to be used as a propaganda tool, showing how a good American can bash a Japanese soldier. Tony told the press his first KO came as a fourteen-year-old when he knocked out a Japanese cook at the Orange Lawn Tennis Club, but he "had to quit eating at the club because I was afraid the bum might poison me." He put on grass skirts and did the hula in a New York floor show and did a quick turn as a bubble dancer, lifting and cavorting with a plastic orb as large as a Shetland pony, in a corny vaudeville act. He was a ready-made sight gag.

With Tami Mauriello and Abe Simon, both heavyweights who lost to Joe Louis, Tony played a bent-nosed thug in *On the Waterfront*. Given the name "Truck," he delivers a line at the beginning of the film when a stool pigeon is thrown off a tenement roof in a dockside union dispute. The line, not clear unless one listens closely, is "the canary could sing but couldn't fly." Then he laughs. Tony appears slightly self-conscious, though physically suited to the role.

Typecast, he played Fingers in *The Best Things in Life Are Free* and took an uncredited turn in the film version of *Guys and Dolls*. In a more substantial part, he played across from Burl Ives in *Wind Across the Everglades*, a movie notable for being Peter Falk's first film credit. Ives's character, Cottonmouth, poaches in the everglades and Tony, as a character named Beef, is his henchman. Directed by Nicholas Ray — who was fired by writer/producer Budd Shulberg before the filming concluded — the movie screened in theaters and drive-ins in 1958. With Christopher Plummer and Gypsy Rose Lee in star turns, the film anticipates the ecological concerns of the next few decades. Burl Ives' Cottonmouth hopes to plunder the bounty of the swamp, while Plummer, an Audubon member, of all things, tries to preserve it.

THAT REMAINED in the future for Tony Galento, far removed from his bout with Louis. The future also held another tavern — not a dive, but one on which he spent four thousand dollars, following plans drafted by Daniel J. Scrocco, an Orange architect. Together they constructed an octagonal bar, 24 feet long and 18 feet wide, and a dining room 30 by 17. The entrance — porcelain enamel and a plate glass set into aluminite — opened onto three lounges. Tony promised a guy could bring his best girl without "her having to worry about getting sawdust in her shoes." The name changed from Tony Galento's Café to Galento's Bar and Grill.

The future held a separation from his wife, Mary, the onset of diabetes, the slow fading of his glory. It held his participation in the Mangia Mangia Club, an Orange eating group that went from restaurant to restaurant, eating, drinking, sampling. It held countless punches in the shoulder, the rap of his fist on a young buck's ribs, the shake-can voice asking, "You know who I am, kid?"

In 1940 it held an invitation from Bruno Mussolini, son of Il Duce and president of the Italian Boxing Federation, to fight during Rome's 1942 World's Fair. Young Mussolini received a letter in reply from Galento, assuring him that Galento would like to lead a delegation of Italian Americans to Rome for the fair. It never materialized.

Eventually the movies stopped calling. In a publicity gag to jog their memories, he campaigned for president as representative of the Prohibition Party. He ran a poker parlor out of his house and brought in some money that way, but eventually the police broke up the party and fined the players ten dollars a piece. The fine served to alert Galento that he could not run the parlor out of his house, though Tony and his pals told the press they "weren't playing for keeps." He had a skirmish with an Orange policeman over a parking problem in front of his tavern, and got hit over the head with a billy club for his efforts. When patrolman James Meehan claimed Tony retaliated with a right cross, Tony blurted that only a sucker leads with a right. He complained that he was being persecuted for being famous, and that he put Orange on the map. Besides, he added, "it's a wonder a guy wouldn't get a break in his own hometown. And especially from the cops. Why, I used to let them slice their own turkey in my kitchen, but I had to put a stop to that one day when we caught one of them back there ripping a bird apart with his hands." The ten-dollar fine for "disorderly conduct" stood.

The future held various stories that circulated about him, the most famous one involving Jackie Gleason, star of *The*

Honeymooners. The story went that one night Gleason received a terrific heckling from a loud drunk in a dinner club. Gleason asked the drunk to step outside. A big man, Gleason knew how to handle himself and saw before him a loud-mouthed blowhard, the type he had knocked around for years. Accounts of the fight are hazy, but nearly all confirm its brevity. Gleason threw a punch and Two Ton threw a punch, and Gleason decided he needed to lie down.

Tony's present and future intersected with a group of California kids who took to the beach and dunes between San Onofre to Point Dume from 1936 to 1942, during the height of Two Ton's fame. A young man named Don James lugged along a camera and photographed the excursions. The physical beauty of the beaches — and the great isolation of the water and sand captured in the sepia photographs — is memorable. Don James's eye for an image would make him famous as a surf photographer, but perhaps nothing he ever did surpassed the series of photographs he snapped at San Onofre. Part of the success of the photographs, which weren't in wide circulation until much later, still in Galento's future, is the twinkle of the young men and women who populate the pictures. Clowning, smoking, surfing, they appear immortal, providing a glimpse of Eden, the world as a younger place. The boys are slim and handsome, and they surf in rows that cut out their images against a bright sky, or they turn somersaults in the surf, their skin — even in black-and-white photographs — tanned to brown honey. Looking at the photographs, one wonders why they ever departed the beach for worldly promises.

And then a photograph of Tony Galento incongruously appears. He stands in a black bathing suit cut like a sarong around his ample hips and belly, his chest hairy, his skin pale, his forehead sloped back to baldness. His left arm is looped around Don James's shoulders and his right hand holds out a tremendous lobster. The caption below the photograph explains that Tony had been reluctant to hold the lobster, and that only great persuasion talked him into it. It is easy to imagine the young men finding Galento a source of humor, a character who wandered improbably into their midst. Next to Don James, who is young and slim and handsome, Tony appears out of place, a foreigner to such leisure and tranquility. The caption identifies Tony as a famous wrestler, but makes no mention of his bout with Louis. That, at least here, was gone.

11

In Wildwood, New Jersey, the seventeenth annual marble tournament became more exciting at about the time the fight concluded. According to the *New York Times,* William Anderson of Atlanta seized first place, having won fifteen consecutive games. His percentage of .767 did not equal some of the better performers — Doug Opperman of Pittsburgh, at .800, or Francis Wellence, of Throop, Pennsylvania, at .867 — but he had a knack for salvaging contests at the last minute. He appeared to be the favorite to win the tournament.

A display at the World's Fair, conceived by the Braille Committee of Passaic, New Jersey's Red Cross, and carried out by the students of Passaic schools, opened at the Community Center of the New York Guild for the

Jewish blind the same evening as the fight. The exhibit, located at 172 East 96th Street, provided a model fair built to one-twentieth scale. A Braille metal tag identified each of the fair's fifteen major buildings, and a Braille map positioned the models according to the original blueprints, lent to the Passaic pupils by the fair management.

IN SAN FRANCISCO, near the start of the fight, two men launched racing pigeons in what they believed to be the first transcontinental pigeon race in American history. Burgess Charles Beckman and Albert Greb, both of Pittsburgh, Pennsylvania, expected the five-year-old pigeons to arrive home in ten days. The birds could fly four hundred to eight hundred miles daily and the trip constituted a twenty-six-hundred-mile flight. The birds, released, caught a significant tailwind almost immediately, a bonus neither man had counted on. They flew away from the sun and swept with the updrafts over the mountains.

TONY LEFT Yankee Stadium with his wife and a flock of supporters and stopped at Dr. Stern's office in Newark, where he told the reporters who had tailed him that he felt pretty good. Dr. Stern used twenty-three stitches to reattach Tony's nose to his cheek, to tidy up his right jaw line and the gash above his left eye, and to suture the flesh of his lips back together. The left side of Tony's face had swollen into a lumpy mash, but Dr. Stern could only apply ice. By the time Tony departed the office, he wore a bright white eyebrow of tape and a goatee of gauze on his chin and cheeks. His face shined the color of pale lamb, a pink, raw shade that made people turn away slightly when they first encountered him. His hands had swollen until the knuckles had disappeared in the gush of immobilizing liquid, and his right ear burned flannel red.

TWO TON smoked a cigar on the way home from Newark. It was late, nearly two in the morning, and the streets lay open and wide and quiet. The train of cars moved crisply through the last part of the June night, the adrenaline of the fight still propelling them to move faster, to arrive, though the main event had concluded. The car tires bounced over trolley lines, passed the leering docks and cranes, the radio conning towers of cargo ships peeking above the lighted horizon.

AT MADAME BEY'S, where Tony had trained, the fireflies flashed on and off near the Watchung Mountains, the shine of New York City a quiet, comforting presence forty or fifty miles distant. The outdoor ring, where during the daylight hours fighters trained beneath a shed roof, dried in the night air. Blood, spilled the day before, turned to copper chips on the pale canvas. Fit men, boxers of all weights and classes — Max Schmeling, Gene Tunney, Mickey Walker, Tony Canzoneri, Kid Gavilan, Rocky Graziano, Kid Chocolate, Ike Williams, Jake LaMotta, Sandy Saddler, and Jersey Joe Walcott all trained at Bey's — snored in slow fatigue, their regimen exacting, their sleep scheduled to the rhythms of the camp.

The remarkable Hranoush Agaganian, better known in boxing lore as Madame Bey — a mezzo-soprano who spoke seven languages and had performed in Carnegie Hall, but who entered American history by standing on stage beside her friend, President McKinley, when a wild-eyed anarchist with the unpronounceable name of Czologsz shot the president at the Buffalo Pan-American Exposition before she could sing the national anthem — slept as well. She did not count Tony Galento among her favorites, and she did not mind terribly that he had lost. She liked Max Schmeling, called him "my Max," but she had listened to the fight with the other boys. It was a shame, she said often, when any of her fighters had to endure the loss of their art. Galento, she understood, trained at her facility only by command from the boxing commission.

Around her the men slept and turned in their beds. They slept in rooms kept deliberately Spartan. To fight potently, one first had to strip away distractions, to grow closer to the earth and the simple fuels of sun and nutrition. At first light the men, ten or twenty of them, would rise and jog through the mountain trails. They would return for breakfasts of plain, simple food — farm eggs and bacon, Jersey milk, perhaps a slice of tomato with a wedge of melon. On their second cup of coffee they would pick up the paper and examine the fight coverage. Some of them would exclaim that Galento almost got him, and others would say it wasn't that close, but either way they read the headlines. They laid the paper out and left it there for anyone to see, the whole story, the tell, and then they wandered back to their rooms for a brief lay-down before the sparring began, the wet, bloody business of gloves and mouthpieces and jocks.

WHEN AT LAST the cars pulled up in front of Tony's tavern, a crowd of several thousand whooped and screamed his name. People rushed forward and tried to put a hand on him as he climbed out of the car. He waved, made a circle with his cigar, then surrendered to the hive of people pushing him inside his bar. Fifty, sixty years later, people would claim that Two Ton Tony Galento was the best thing, the most famous thing, to ever come out of Orange, New Jersey. Lou Costello, the great comedian, had sometimes mistakenly been awarded to Orange, but he had been from a few towns over, not far, but not Orange. The greatest night in Orange history, some citizens contended, rode on Tony's shoulders. The highest moment of national regard.

True or not, a roar from the seven hundred remaining customers stuffed the room when Tony finally stepped into his tavern. He paused, for an instant nonplussed by the attention, by the knowledge that he had not won and that now, as kindly as it was meant, the congratulations came tinged with consolation. But it was not in his nature to sulk. Hands pushed him forward. He resisted only long enough to rock back on his heels and cup his hands around his mouth, then gave a high, warbling Tarzan yodel that sent the crowd slapping one another on the shoulder, joy grabbing a surer grip in the room.

He glad-handed his way around the bar, drank a beer, yodeled like Tarzan a few more times, yelled he had been robbed. He promised to reporters he would flatten Louis the next time he fought him. He claimed Louis couldn't take a punch. He had already begun to misremember the left jab that smashed his face flat for four rounds. He wanted Louis again, he told anyone who would listen. Next time, he said. Then he grabbed a fistful of bills from the cash register, waved again to the crowd, and disappeared.

JOE JACOBS scrambled to a back room in the tavern, his titanic tongue still wagging. Not three hours after the fight concluded, he began the drumbeat for a rematch in September.

"I know we gave out reports that Tony was training hard," Jacobs said, his hair mussed and his arms still pumping the air, "but it's over now and we can tell the truth. That Galento is a marvel. He didn't train. He was drinking, smoking great big cigars and going to bed at one and two o'clock in the morning. I know we said he was in bed early at night, but he used to sneak out of camp and do everything he ever did before. If Galento almost beat Louis when he was in that condition, imagine what he would do if I really got him to train. Galento licked himself — Louis didn't beat him. If I can get another Louis match for September, I promise you that Galento will be the next champion."

THE REPORTERS left. The crowd peeled away. Customers had consumed seven kegs of beer, a record for the tavern. Mary Grasso, Tony's wife, closed the tavern around three, moving through the established routine while still wearing the dress she wore to the fight. She also closed the door on the biggest day in her husband's life. Everything he did, or said, or attempted from that point forward would be traced back to the eleven minutes in Yankee Stadium. Champion of the world for two seconds. That's what people said. Champ of the waterfront, of New Jersey, of the black bastards who pushed in from every side, of every Italian living in the world at that precise moment, champ of all that.

If she could have put it into words, she might have remarked that it was a rare thing to be able to pinpoint with certainty the pinnacle of a man's life, but that her husband's moment lay behind him now appeared as obvious as salt.

Mary Grasso knew only a little of what was to come. Her feet hurt and she had a mild headache. She locked the tavern door and turned out the lights. Orange, New Jersey, had gone to bed at last. The bakers' lights had already come on, and she smelled fresh bread as she walked home, the sound of her heels echoing against the building fronts.

AT ABOUT the same time the tide turned at Sandy Hook and Barnegat Bay. Sunrise on June 29 came at 4:26, and the first beams of light hit the New Jersey shore. Water pushed on the sand, and the light shucked the waves in ringlets to its highest edge, leaving kelp and seaweed and a few severed crab legs to mark the tidal line. Gulls lifted from their perches and banked into the air. They turned and hung like seeds thrown into the wind and carried to the earth.

* * *

WHEN A FEW friends stopped over at Tony Galento's house near dawn, they found him in the kitchen, money spread out before him, slowly counting the day's tavern receipts. It came out to $255, but Tony needed the sum recounted by his friend and sometime-manager, Herman Muggsy Taylor. He found it difficult to concentrate; his head still carried the ding dong of the Bomber's blows. Wearing a white T-shirt, Two Ton smoked a cigar and drank a beer. Moths hit at the window screens. The New Jersey night had turned cool and gentle. The sun, the visitors all knew, would rise soon. Sitting in his kitchen, his child asleep in the rooms above him, his income secure, his future promising, Tony Galento felt brittle and tired and at peace. Maybe Mary, back from the tavern, fixed a sandwich for him. Maybe his brother, Russell, smoked a cigarette across the table, the curl of smoke wrapping around the fluorescent kitchen light. The next day — although none of them could anticipate the gush of interest — he would entertain offers from around the country. The phone would ring all day; telegrams would pour in from fighters and promoters all over the nation. For now, though, the coolness of the table, the click of the tile floor when the dog walked across it, the scatter of the locust trees outside, proved sufficient.

Naturally someone mentioned Louis. Someone would always mention Louis from now on, but Galento could not know it then. Louis, they understood, had already signed to fight Bob Pastor, a slugger he had beaten in a listless affair in 1937, a few fights before he had won the heavyweight championship. The fight, a homecoming for Louis, was scheduled for Briggs Stadium in Detroit. To make it a special event, the managers booked it for twenty rounds, the first twenty-round championship fight since Jess Willard beat Jack Johnson in Cuba after twenty-six rounds. Louis had also signed to fight Arturo Godoy in February 1940. If Galento wanted another go at Louis, he had to stand in line. He also needed to beat Lou Nova, the most highly touted young heavyweight on the scene.

In the days that followed, Galento and Nova signed for a bout in Philadelphia's Municipal Stadium in September. The winner of the bout, newspapers reported, would meet Louis the following June. A 1 to 3 underdog, Tony would fight a vicious bout in front of twenty thousand screaming fans who had paid seventy-five thousand dollars in receipts. Reporters called the fight a barroom brawl, a blood match. Both fighters sustained cuts in the early rounds, and blood followed their fists back and forth. Galento's thumb gouged Nova's left eye so badly that Nova required surgery afterward. In the ninth round ringside fans shouted to the ref to stop the contest. In the fourteenth round, Galento floored Nova twice. Nova rose to his feet, defenseless, his hands at his sides. Galento motioned for the referee, George Blake, to intervene, and finally the referee did. It was a fight, some people said, to make a dog turn away.

The victory over Nova was Galento's last significant victory. He endured beatings by the Baer brothers — Max and Buddy — and then slowly moved on to his brief career in the movies. He never got another shot at Louis. His real career, his one great trick, remained the job of being Two Ton Tony Galento.

But he could not know that at the end of a June night in 1939. Instead he retired to his bedroom, his bandages white, his body exhausted. He lay in the quiet house, his hands throbbing, morning light climbing out of the ocean. As he fell asleep perhaps his body jerked in memory of what it had endured, and perhaps this time he did not fall, but stood in those two splendid seconds forever, champ of the world, the man who lifted Joe Louis from the earth.

Acknowledgments

IN LOOKING BACK into Tony Galento's life and time, I have been assisted by many people and many splendid works. I am indebted to the hundreds of reporters who covered the fights of the 1930s, especially William Ratner of the *Newark News Ledger,* whose *Punching the Bag* column was a wonderful attic jammed with memories of the Laurel Garden, the Elizabeth Armory, and wrestlers with names like Little Wolf. Columnist John Kieran of the *New York Times* provided commentary and background. So did other columnists of the day: Bill Henry, Arch Ward, Bob Considine, Bob Ray, and Shirley Povitch. Nat Bodian, a longtime reporter for the *Newark News*, gave countless hours of advice and tips. His excellent Web site, Old Newark Memories, pointed me in all the right directions. Nat Bodian also shocked me by reminiscing about the bicycle training he did on New Jersey's route 22, now one of the nation's most crowded highways. The memories and details he provided gave life to my research.

As a chronological narrative of Tony Galento's career, Joseph G. Donovan's *Galento the Great,* published shortly before the Louis bout, helped me more than I can say. Assembled quickly to present Galento to the American public, *Galento the Great* nevertheless captured a time and place and gave me an outline and chronology for Galento's life that I might not have found otherwise. Typing with two fingers on an old manual machine, Joseph Donovan was, according to men who knew him, a Damon Runyan figure, a 1930s journalist type complete with striped shirt, silk waistcoat, and the requisite cigar. He wrote for years at the *Newark Morning Ledger* and delivered wonderful prose five times a week.

No one can read about Joe Louis without coming to admire the man. Fortunately his life and career have been documented by several superb writers, and I have learned from all of them. His autobiography, *My Life,* written with Edna Rust and Art Rust Jr., is a marvel of frankness. Although boxing fans may disagree with my depiction of Louis as a boxer, his contribution as a man to our nation is beyond second guessing. No athlete has broken so many social barriers, and done so with such consummate grace, as Joe Louis. His fights in the ring remain the least of his battles.

Mildred Galento, married to Tony's brother, Russell, attended the Louis–Galento fight in Yankee Stadium. She also stayed in Tony's Diamond Mirror Cocktail Lounge afterward, waiting for Tony to appear. She knew Tony and spoke frankly about him. She did not pretend he was less than a difficult man, but her innate fairness permitted her to render a full accounting of her interactions with him. I am grateful that she willingly spoke to a stranger, and I hope her words are fairly represented in this book.

Tony Monica provided me with pictures and a personal tour of his beloved Orange, New Jersey. He also introduced me to several older gentlemen who sparred with, or knew, Tony Galento in the 1930s. Tony Monica still lives in Orange and can still show you where to get a good sausage sandwich. His photo-documentary work on Orange has informed my research in countless ways.

I appreciate the contribution of Harry Schaffer, whose excellent boxing memorabilia Web site, combined with his generous willingness to correspond, gave me a final run-through for this book. He checked my boxing history. For taking time to speak with me on the phone, thanks to Lou Duva and Bert Sugar and Jerry Izenberg. Thanks also go to Michael Immerso, whose book on Newark's First District is terrific.

To Alan Lelchuk, who brought the book to Steerforth Press and has always been an inspiration, thanks many times over. Thanks to the fine staff at Steerforth, especially my editor, Chip Fleischer.

Thanks, also, to Joyce Bruce at Plymouth State University for her help with interlibrary loans, and to the research librarians at Dartmouth College who gave me access to the *New York Times* and many other periodicals. To my wife, Wendy, and to my son, Justin, thanks for listening to all the boxing stories. To anyone I may have forgotten to thank or to cite, I apologize. I have done my best to honor the work you contributed to this topic.

Notes on Sources

Preface

The information in the preface and in many subsequent chapters derives from various newspaper accounts of the fight. Because its archives are the most complete, the *New York Times* served as my paper of record. Often a second newspaper account confirmed my original reading of an event. Whenever possible, I cited the newspaper and the reporter when employing a quote.

Chapter 1

The suggestion that Joe Louis had already engaged in affairs with white women by the time he won the heavyweight title in 1937 from Braddock comes from his autobiography, *My Life*, written with Edna Rust and Art Rust Jr. The note from the southern preacher imploring Joe Louis to be "a black man outside, but a white man inside," appeared in *Joe Louis: American* by Margery Miller. Details about Yankee Stadium and its construction came from *Ballparks of North America*, by Michael

Benson and from *Yankee Stadium: 75 Years of Drama and Glory* by Robinson and Jennison. Tony Galento's statement about Abe Feldman and fighting below "the equator" came from a variety of newspaper sources. Because some controversy exists concerning Max Schmeling's reaction to the death of Tom O'Rourke when O'Rourke visited Schmeling and Galento before their respective bouts with Louis and Al Gainer, it should be noted my mention comes directly from Joseph Donovan's rendering of the event in *Galento the Great*.

Chapter 2

Information about a boxer's hand and the force it exerts on an opponent derived from research performed by two astronauts, Stephen Wilk and Ronald McNair, who died tragically in the *Challenger* accident in 1986. Using strobe lights, they calculated the speed of various karate blows. The effect of the hands on a boxer's health — the injuries, the potential risks to a fighter — came from a number of sources, but primarily from Web sites dedicated to boxing injuries. Joyce Carol Oates asserts in her excellent book *On Boxing* that a heavyweight's punch may deliver ten thousand pounds of force and that the brain must absorb part of the impact in its jelly sac. The description of Galento biting his tongue in half came from Donovan's *Galento the Great*. The account of Joe Louis's descent into mental illness comes from Barney Nagler's *Brown Bomber: The Pilgrimage of Joe Louis*.

Chapter 3

Jack Milley's wonderful description of Galento first appeared in *Collier's Weekly*. The information about Gene Tunney's proposal that Galento fight Gargantua came from Tunney's [illegible]olumns on the matter in the *Connecticut Nutmeg*.

Chapter 4

The information about the Galento family's immigration from Italy comes from Donovan's *Galento the Great*. Background information about the general movement of Italians to the west comes from the introduction to the excellent boxing book *The Italian Stallions*, by Thomas Hauser and Stephen Brunt, who also pointed me toward Jake LaMotta's stunning description of tenement life made famous in *Raging Bull*. The description of street life in an Italian neighborhood derives from Michael Immerso's account of Newark's First Ward. Information about New York during the 1930s and the effects of the Depression come from the reference *American Decades*. Details about the ice business in Orange and elsewhere came from *Galento the Great* and other articles.

Chapter 5

The descriptions in this chapter derive entirely from newspaper accounts. *Heroes Without a Country*, Donald McRae's excellent book about Joe Louis and Jesse Owens, proved a wonderful source for many things in this work. In this chapter the information about Joe Louis's visit to Harlem after he defeated Carnera derives from that account.

Chapter 6

The second poem in this chapter comes from the *Newark Star-Ledger*'s sports pages. Information on John Roxborough, Julian Black, and Chappie Blackburn comes from a variety of sources, primarily newspaper accounts. Blackburn, more than the others, is controversial because of his criminal record. Accounts vary concerning the specified charges; the truth or falsehood of those charges rest out of the purview of this book. A.J. Leibling described Whitey Bimstein in his boxing features.

Chapter 7

Information on Mun Barrow and Searcy Hospital in Alabama comes from *Searcy: Past, Present and Future*, by Belinda Jones, Public Information, April 30, 1979. The information on Al Jolson and Hillcrest Golf Club comes from his autobiography, *My Life*. I first read about the tailor Billy Taub, and the Louis' purchases there, in Donald McCrae's *Heroes Without a Country*. The suggestion that boxers acted as the standar bearers for men trapped in the dullness of industrialized Depression America comes from Elliott J. Gorn's *The Manly Art*.

Chapter 8

The description of the Galento family at the end of the bout derives from interviews with Mildred Galento and newspaper accounts of the fight.

Chapter 9

The Tony Galento polka, played at wrestling matches, appeared in William Ratner's column in the *Star-Ledger*.

Chapter 10

Information in this chapter derives from newspaper accounts of the bout.

Chapter 11

Accounts of the aftermath of the fight derive from newspaper reports and interviews with Mildred Galento.

Bibliography

Anderson, Frederick. *Bicycling, A History*. New York and Washington: Praeger, 1972.

Benson, Michael. *Ballparks of North America*. Jefferson, N.C.: McFarland & Company, 1989.

Collins, Nigel. *Boxing Babylon*, Secaucus, N.J.: Citadel Press, 1990.

Cotsonika, Nicholas. "When Joe Louis Fought, the Country Came to a Halt." *Detroit Free Press.*

Donovan, Joseph. *Galento the Great.* New York: George Winn, 1939.

Glendinning, Richard and Sally. *Gargantua, the Mighty Gorilla*. Champaign, Illinois: Garrard, 1974.

Gorn, Elliott. *The Manly Art*. Ithaca, New York: Cornell University Press, 1986.

Hageman, Robert. "Madame Bey's — Training Camp for Champion Prizefighters." In *The Historian*, The Newsletter of the Summit Historical Society, September 2003.

Hauser, Thomas, Stephen Brunt, and Michael Silver, eds. *The Italian Stallions: Heroes from the Prime of Boxing's Life*. Wilmington, Del.: SportClassic Books, 2003.

Helliwell, Arthur. *The Private Lives of Famous Fighters*. London: Cendric Day, 1949.

Hodes, Robert. *Tarzan of the Apes*. Original text by Edgar Rice Burroughs. New York: Watson-Guptill, 1972.

Immerso, Michael. *Newark's Little Italy*. Newark, New Jersey: Rutgers University Press and Newark Public Library, 1997.

Jones, Belinda. *Searcy: Past, Present and Future*. Public Information, April 30, 1979.

Kahn, Roger. A *Flame of Pure Fire*. New York: Harcourt Brace, 1999.

LaMotta, Jake, with Peter Savage and Joseph Carter. *Raging Bull*. Englewood Cliffs, New Jersey: Prentice-Hall International, 1970.

Lamparski, Richard. *Whatever Became Of*... Fifth Series. New York: Crown, 1974.

Lardner, Rex. *Ten Heroes of the Twenties*. New York: G.P. Putnam's Sons, 1966.

Liebling, A.J. *Just Enough Liebling*. New York: North Point Press, 2004.

——. *The Sweet Science*. New York: Viking Press, 1956.

Lintz, Gertrude. *Animals Are My Hobby*. New York: Robert McBride, 1942.

McCrae, Donald. *Heroes Without a Country*. New York: Ecco Press, 2003.

Miller, Margery. *Joe Louis: American*. New York: A. A. Wyn, 1945.

North, Henry Ringling, and Alden Hatch. *The Circus Kings*. Garden City, New York: Doubleday, 1960.

Oates, Joyce Carol. *On Boxing*. Garden City, New York: Dolphin/Doubleday, 1987.

Remnick, David. *King of the World*. New York: Random House, 1998.

Robinson, Ray, and Christopher Jennison. *Yankee Stadium*. New York: Penguin, 1998.

Samuels, Charles. *The Magnificent Rube*. New York: McGraw-Hill, 1957.

Schmeling, Max. *Max Schmeling: An Autobiography*. George B. von der Lippe, trans. Chicago: Bonus Books, 1998.

Tompkins, Vincent, ed. *American Decades, 1930–1939*. Detroit: Gale Research, 1995.

Tunney, Gene. "*Gorilla vs. Man.*" *Connecticut Nutmeg*, vol. 1, no. 3; June 1938.

Walker, Mickey. *Will to Conquer*. Hollywood, California: House-Warven, 1953.

Wilson, Peter. *Ringside Seat*. New York: Rich and Cowan, 1940.